A SHORT SYSTEMATIC THEOLOGY

A Short Systematic Theology

PAUL F. M. ZAHL

WILLIAM B. EERDMANS PUBLISHING COMPANY
GRAND RAPIDS, MICHIGAN / CAMBRIDGE, U.K.

Wm. B. Eerdmans Publishing Co.

255 Jefferson Ave. S.E., Grand Rapids, Michigan 49503 /
P.O. Box 163, Cambridge CB3 9PU U.K.

Printed in the United States of America

05 04 03 02 01 00   7 6 5 4 3 2 1

Library of Congress Cataloging-in-Publication Data

Zahl, Paul F. M.

A short systematic theology / Paul F. M. Zahl.

p.   cm.

Includes bibliographical references and indexes.

ISBN 0-8028-4729-3 (alk. paper)

1. Theology, Doctrinal.   I. Title.

BT75.2.Z27   2000

230 — dc21

00-063601

www.eerdmans.com

This book is dedicated to
Mary,
my beloved wife

Contents

CONTENTS

Introduction

Theodore Beza (1519-1605) said that the whole of Christian theology could be condensed on a single sheet of paper. He did this, and it remains an epigrammatic touchstone for all who come after him (see Appendix A). Karl Barth (1886-1968) tried to do one better: he said that his theology, all fourteen volumes of it, could be condensed on one *half* of a sheet of paper. Barth never produced the page.

Brevity is a virtue in most things. Chekhov said that "brevity is the brother of brilliance." Jesus demonstrated this in the Lord's Prayer and in the Beatitudes. Dickens displayed the virtue of brevity in *A Christmas Carol*, which can be read aloud in one sitting. Milton's sonnets are masterpieces of theological reflection distilled to fourteen lines.

Short is better. In all of rock 'n' roll, no one has ever produced a better single than "Can't Explain" by the Who (1964). How long is it? It is exactly two minutes and three seconds long. In the information avalanche overwhelming the world in bewildering forms, short is better. It really is. "For God is in heaven, and you upon earth; therefore let your words be few" (Ecclesiastes 5:2).

The New Testament is very short. Without any cuts, it can be carried in your pocket, even your vest pocket. The Book of Common Prayer (1928) is also very short, and the same applies. The truth, while inexhaustible in its applications in individual situations, can be expressed in short form.

A principal feature of this systematic theology of the Christian religion is its brevity. There is no need for padding. There is also no need for this theology to be exhaustive, although it is complete. The reader can think through for himself or herself the implications of the main ideas. The Prologue to the Gospel of St. John is eighteen verses. Yet it tells you everything you need to know about God in his relation to the human race. The eighteen verses are not exhaustive, but they are complete. Their implications are inexhaustible.

In this systematic theology I seek to give the basic points of Christian theology in three chapters. The first chapter gives the subject of theology, the God who is speaking as Subject. The second chapter gives the content of theology, the organizing principle behind which is the atonement of Christ. The third chapter gives the method of theology, which is the intellectual freedom to criticize the text (i.e., the Bible). This quality of intellectual freedom is connected to self-criticism, which is another word for the biblical idea of repentance. Self-criticism roots the method of theology in humility before God, theology's Subject.

In theology, everything hinges on the starting point. The starting point for Christian theology is the "Old, Old Story" of Christ's appearance in world history. World history, theologically speaking, is centuries and centuries of theater, dramatized by millions of actors but featuring two main characters, Christ and Satan. A few principles of interpretation are sufficient to portray the human story and the interactions of God and Satan within that story.

Every theology that has ever existed carries a prism through which the data, in particular the Bible data, are organized. This particular theology has three such prisms: the principle of Jesus' continuity or continued life through to the present day; the principle of atonement; and the principle of intellectual freedom rooted in self-criticism.

The reader should find the basics here of story and of method, from the creation of the world right through to the conclusion of world history. That this theology is Bible-based should be clear from the start.

To provide a teaching tool, I wish to view the theology of the Christian religion as expressed tersely in a cycle of works created by Lucas Cranach (1472-1553) in the early Reformation period. These drawings, prints, and paintings depict the gospel message in shorthand. The artist seeks to develop his own shorthand for the whole sweep of the Old Testament and New Testament message, and he seeks to do this in one visual image. That Cranach was able to achieve this reflects his genius for composition. It also reflects the fact that the biblical story of God's engagement with the human race is easily understandable.

This little book is written in the style of Cranach's 1529 woodcut entitled "The Old and New Testament" (see Appendix B). Cranach's woodcut is an unparalleled example of close and dense theological expression rendered visually. This systematic theology attempts also to put the whole story into one short, readable scroll. Then, just as the artist painted himself into the picture in the final version from 1559, I try to set the reader of the scroll within it.

To present the ideas of this systematic theology within a brief one-volume whole, I have chosen the old method of thesis and explanation. The three chapters of the book consist of twenty-five theses. Each thesis is accompanied by a short exposition, either before it or after it. The twenty-five theses outline the subject, the content, and the method of theology from which all subsidiary themes and all applications can be developed.

I would like to thank Mrs. Nita Moorhead for her tireless assistance in the production of this book.

CHAPTER ONE

The Subject of Theology: Jesus Christ

For Christians, the prism through which all light concerning God is reflected is Jesus Christ. This means that *Christology* is the beginning and the end, better, the starting point and summary, of all Christian thought. Christology is Paul's theme when he writes, "For it is the very God who said, 'Let light shine out of darkness,' who has shone in our hearts to give the light of the knowledge of the glory of God in the face of Christ" (2 Corinthians 4:6). Christology is the subject of theology. More precisely put, Jesus Christ is the subject of theology.

We understand that God in any sense differentiated from Jesus Christ is unknowable. This needs to be affirmed from the start. John writes in the prologue to his Gospel, "No one has ever seen God; the only Son, who is in the bosom of the Father, he has made him known" (1:18). John repeats this idea forcefully in his first letter: "No one has ever seen God" (4:12). Job complains of God, "Oh, that I knew where I might find him, that I might come even to his seat!" (23:3). Bible religion knows nothing about a God who can be found or made out from our side of things. "Such knowledge is too wonderful; it is high, I cannot attain it" (Psalm 139:6).

Why is theology unable to start from God as the creator of the universe, or God as the "ground of our being," or God simply as the Other? Theology is unable to start in those places because the picture of God that emerges from such beginnings is speculative.

5

It is speculation, for example, that there exists a "first cause" that set all things in motion. No proof! It is speculation that there is an underlying principle governing or sustaining all that is. No proof! It is speculation that otherness — that is, all that is other to me as the subject of my life — has any personal or conscious character. No proof! It is speculation to suggest that a single entity, power, or unity created the universe, even in some pre-existing sense. In that case, the case that there is a unity or fundamental harmony to the natural world, there exists *proof to the contrary*. There is contrary, discouraging evidence against the existence of a unified primordial harmony. The contrary evidence is the cruelty of nature, the catastrophes of nature, the predatory character of the food chain from top to bottom, the disorder of nature, and the demonstrated fact of Heisenberg's uncertainty principle. Nature is neither orderly nor pre-existing nor absolute nor kind.

We go wrong from the beginning if we start with God in any other sense than as known in concrete engagement with universal human vulnerability. We go wrong if we start from a god who exists detached from our experience of relentless, arbitrary, even cruel nature. God cannot exist apart from the Lisbon earthquake of 1755 or Hurricane Mitch in 1998.

We also go wrong in starting with God in any metaphysical or ontological remove from the empirical lives we live in the world. This is because of the existence of sin within these empirical lives. The theme of sin, its verifiability among all sorts and conditions of men and women, through all moments of recorded history, prevents us from positing a God who exists in any stage of his existence apart even for a moment or an atom from the problem of sin. Because of the ubiquity of injustice and sin in the world, no God can exist who is not a moral being. We have this written in our human nature by the instrument of conscience. "What the law requires is written on the hearts [of human beings], while their conscience also bears witness and their conflicting thoughts accuse or perhaps excuse them on that day when, according to my gospel, God judges the secrets of men by Christ Jesus" (Romans 2:15-16). Plain experience and common sense inform us that no abstract Person can have made us *as we are*, let alone endured us, without also wishing to delete us and start over (Genesis 8:21; Zephaniah 1:2). Therefore, the existence of cruel and arbitrary nature, together with the universality of human sin, prevents us from beginning the theological enterprise from any concept of God that is distinct from revelation. All theologies of a cosmic harmonic principle shipwreck on the truths of tragedy, catastrophe, and injustice.

This is why Christian theology is Christology and why the subject of theology is Christ. Moreover, Christ is theology's subject not only as its theme but also in the sense of being its governor or voice, its driver. Christ proves to be the "I" of the conversation between God and human nature. God addresses humanity through Christ. He is the subject of address, and we are the object.

Thesis 1: Theology is Christology.

Systematic theology proceeds from an assertion concerning human nature that is not the *Also Sprach Zarathustra* (as in the film *2001*) declared through the first verse of Genesis. We do not start, save in long retrospect, with article 1 of the church's creeds: "I believe in God the Father." Rather, our starting point is article 2: "I believe in Jesus Christ, his only Son, our Lord."

Christian theology is rightly described as being "from the bottom up" rather than "from the top down." The usual contemporary meaning of the phrase "theology from the bottom up" is theology from the vantage point of human experience, through which, partly by observation and partly by analogy, we are able to build up a picture of God, layer by layer. On the other hand, the usual contemporary meaning of the phrase "theology from the top down" is theology that starts from revealed statements about God from God. God from the top down is over and above and also prior to human experience.

A theology that is Christology before it is anything else is a theology from the bottom up. It begins with the existence and ministry of Jesus in his own time and space, and it states that it is *entirely agnostic* concerning anything other than what he has given us to know of the essential attributes of God. We do not know God, nor have we seen him. Even Moses the Lawgiver saw him only "from the back" (Exodus 33:23). Our own subjective visions of God, our personal stories and experiences, are simply whatever they are worth. They are all tarred by the facts of universal self-interestedness, that is, sin, and by the capricious catastrophes of life that we have experienced. We cannot know God from nature or, most especially, from human nature. This will affect our view of mysticism and all attempts to transcend the circumstances of life in order to "find" God. We "look for another" (Matthew 11:3), that is, another than the god or gods to be observed in nature or within ourselves.

Theology is therefore reluctant from the start to speak of God by analogy to any human situations until we first have our feet on the ground. For us that means a close attention to the Jesus of history, the one who "came down to earth from heaven" (Cecil Francis Alexander). Without a word to us who live here, without a word to us who experience the disasters of creation gone wrong in the world around us and in the world within us, theology is only speculation and projection.

Ludwig Feuerbach (1804-1872) understood the basic mistake of all theologies that start from the bottom up as that idea is generally understood today. He saw that theology as conceived by the human being is anthropology writ large. Mystified by the overwhelming enigma of human nature, we fantasize a god or gods to fill our perceived needs. The shape of God is the shape of our unmet yearnings. Barth and others in the so-called neo-orthodox school of thought slammed Feuerbach while admitting some of the truth of his critique. We require revelation, the neo-orthodox theologians said, a Word from outside ourselves, in order to speak about God. He is silent unless he chooses to speak. All attempts to "feel after" God from our end are destined to fail (Proverbs 1:28; Ecclesiastes 7:28; Isaiah 41:12; Hosea 5:6; Amos 8:12). They create only the projected idols of our deepest needs and wishes. Feuerbach was surely right about anthropology become theology (i.e., theology from the bottom up), and Barth was surely right about theology from the top down, the Word that alone carries the weight of externally defined truth.

But Barth did not start with Jesus. He started with the electing or sovereign God who said "Let there be light!" and there was light (Genesis

1:3). He started with God's electing choice in general rather than God's grace in Christ in particular. Barth's God was *too* removed, too other. This is because we live here! We see what we see, and we hear what we hear. We feel what we feel. The God who speaks must also be the God who is heard. We are therefore neither Feuerbach's disciples nor Barth's. We understand a different text to be the starting point for systematic theology: "No one has ascended into heaven but he who descended from heaven, the Son of man" (John 3:13).

We understand theology as starting from the ground up, but understand that ground to be Year Zero of the Christian era, the initiating point when Jesus was born into a contentious, eruptive province of the Roman Empire, when "in those days a decree went out from Caesar Augustus that all the world should be taxed" (Luke 2:1). We begin, therefore, christologically, with a concrete historic figure who appeared on the stage of human history. "God's grace is only manifest in the historical work of the historical Christ."[1]

Human History as Theater

Human experience is a theater of endless repetition. It serves as the background for the birth of Christ, which took place *not* "long, long ago in a galaxy far, far away" but rather in a particular province and city governed by the well-documented Roman emperor Augustus (27 B.C.–A.D. 14). Into the cyclical, recidivistic, ever-turning wheel of history came a unique appearance that caused all earlier explanations of the human tragedy — which is also the human comedy if you prefer to see it with irony and fatalism — to recede into the background in favor of a more lucid diagnosis. The Christology of our theology, the starting point for all further reflection, begins with the appearance of one man.

How is it that human history prior to Christ, and in a lesser but still continuing sense after him, is a never-ending cycle of repeated dramas in which each new generation repeats its part and then gives way to the

1. Adolph von Harnack, *History of Dogma*, vol. 7 (New York: Dover, 1961), p. 198.

next? How is it that human history is like a long-running musical in which the actors change every year but the songs remain the same? Like *The Fantasticks* off Broadway or *The Mouse Trap* in London, this play goes on and on. The Bible teaches that history, and in particular every human character within history, exists as a phenomenon of repetition:

> Vanity of vanity, says the Preacher! All is vanity. . . . A generation goes, and a generation comes, but the earth remains for ever. . . . What has been is what will be, and what has been done is what will be done; and there is nothing new under the sun. (Ecclesiastes 1:1, 4, 9)

The same observation concerning the human destiny of endless repetition is offered by Shakespeare in a famous speech from *Macbeth*:

> Tomorrow, and tomorrow, and tomorrow
> Creeps in this petty pace from day to day,
> To the last syllable of recorded time,
> And all our yesterdays have lighted fools
> The way to dusty death. Out, out, brief candle!
> Life's but a walking shadow, a poor player
> That struts and frets his hour upon the stage
> And then is heard no more. It is a tale
> Told by an idiot, full of sound and fury,
> Signifying nothing.
>
> (Act 5, sc. 5, ll. 19-28)

It is vital for theology to recognize and accept the closed system of human history *into which Christ came*. Human history is closed because of the enigmatic and unknowable God who is veiled by the capriciousness of nature and by the permanence and universality of sin.

Human history is also a closed system because of the relentless reality of death, the termination of life. The Preacher of Ecclesiastes, William Shakespeare, and the American poet Edgar Allan Poe all stand speechless before the futile achievement of the world's "works and days" (Hesiod, fourth century B.C.). Poe thus opens our eyes, only to close them forever:

Out — out are the lights — out all!
    And, over each quivering form,
The curtain, a funeral pall,
    Comes down with the rush of a storm,
While the angels, all pallid and wan,
    Uprising, unveiling, affirm
That the play is the tragedy, "Man,"
    And its hero the Conqueror Worm.

We shall return to this theme of human existence as repetitive theater. Jesus Christ is the one who interrupts the never-ending performance of the drama of despair. He turns life as a play of marionettes into life as action and will, life as reality, and life as liberty. He also awakens the dormant vigor of another actor, God's adversary and ours: Satan.

The biblical thinker who most securely explores this unknown landscape, the surveying of which maps out the territory into which Christ came, is St. Paul. Paul's most famous testament of the case of human impotence, the impotence to fundamentally alter the inner as well as the outer geography of human life, occurs in the Book of Romans. Because this standard text (sharpened to its edge in 7:4-24) for understanding the world as the cyclical scenario of the bound, the theater of servitude and not the theater of freedom and life, is so devastating to human hopes of self-generated change, it has attracted to itself a vast and almost undocumentable wealth of discussion in the history of theology. Many, especially in the modern era, have challenged its relentlessly unsettling depiction of human ethical gridlock, the paralysis involved in trying to make a moral choice. Paul's plain meaning, which resonates beyond almost all other passages of Scripture to hearers of every time, every place, every condition, is exactly what he says:

I do not understand my own actions. For I do not do what I want, but I do the very thing I hate. . . . I know that nothing good dwells within me, that is, in my flesh. I can will what is right, but I cannot do it. For I do not do the good I want, but the evil I do not want is what I do. . . . For I delight in the law of God, in my inmost self, but I see in my members another law at war with the law of my mind and making me captive to the law of sin which dwells in my members. Wretched man that I am! Who will deliver me from this body of death? (7:15, 18-19, 22-24)

The twentieth-century philosopher Hannah Arendt (1906-1975) saw this passage from Romans as marking a point of important new discovery in the history of human self-observation: "The Apostle Paul's discovery, which he describes in great detail in the Letter to the Romans, concerns a two-in-one, but these two are not friends or partners; they are in constant struggle with each other. The will, split and automatically producing its own counter-will, is in need of being healed, of becoming one again."

The will is impotent, not because of something outside that prevents willing from succeeding, but because the will hinders itself. Arendt continues,

In the Letter to the Romans, Paul describes an inner experience, the experience of the I-will-and-I-cannot. This experience, followed by the experience of God's mercy, is overwhelming. He explains what happened to him and tells us how and why the two occurrences are interconnected. In the course of the explanation he develops the first comprehensive theory of history, of what history is all about, and he lays the foundations of Christian doctrine.[2]

Paul's painful portrait of human inward dividedness has never been refuted. It has never been countered by any enduring feats of human progress. It has never been disproven by means of any lasting achievement of unity, in which the willing, acting, thinking, and feeling of a person, not to mention a unity of imagining and fantasizing, cohere with the person's thinking and acting. Experience confirms Paul's diagnosis hourly. Experience confirms Paul's diagnosis every sixty seconds!

For the Christian theologian the repetitive, hence static character of

2. Hannah Arendt, "The Apostle Paul and the Impotence of the Will," in part 2 of *The Life of the Mind* (New York: Harcourt Brace & Company, 1978), pp. 64, 70, and 73.

world history is interrupted by the appearance of Christ. The Old Testament worldview foreshadows this interruption through the growing conviction that a Messiah or Savior will come to rescue the people and restore them to a Promised Land. The Old Testament also clings to the conviction that God has interrupted the turning wheel of repeating works and days by means of the exodus of Israel from its bondage in Egypt. The Old Testament worldview is future oriented by virtue of the annually celebrated remembrance of the one great past discontinuity, the exodus under Moses. The ancient and historic discontinuity could occur again! The coming of a future Savior or Christ is therefore spoken by the prophets. The theme comes to a full crescendo in the crisis with Rome resulting in the fall of Jerusalem to Pompey in 63 B.C. This was an unimaginably disappointing catastrophe. It marked the destruction of prophetically inspired hopes for an independent God-enabled state. Nevertheless, the coming of Jesus in 4 B.C. is preceded by the prophetic Jewish belief that history *will* be interrupted, once and for all, by the discontinuous God who interrupted it once before, in the first Passover.

For the early Christians, who drew not only on Jewish messianism but also on deeply felt ideas of fatalism and nihilism that appear in every culture in the face of the repetition-compulsion of history, the starting point for humanity's new age was the appearance of Christ. For the early Christians, Christ transformed the shadow-play and repetitive theater of common existence into the material of human freedom and progress.

Who was Jesus Christ? What was his unique contribution to the human attempt to explain the world, as well as the human attempt to break free from its repetitive hold on everyone who has ever lived? The question is divided into two parts: (1) Who was Jesus historically? and (2) Who is Jesus to the present generation? Who was Jesus then, and who is Jesus now?

The Historical Jesus

The historical Jesus (4 B.C.–29 A.D.) was a Jewish rabbi whose uniqueness consists in his teachings, in his associations during his life, and in the manner of his death. We shall also speak of his resurrection from the dead, referring to the conviction among the students who had accompanied him throughout his work that he appeared to them in the flesh after his burial at Jerusalem.

It is common to speak of St. Paul as if he invented the Christian religion, taking a teacher of wisdom, Jesus, and preaching that teacher into a Savior, the hoped-for Messiah of Israel. This is not true. What becomes clear again and again in the study of Jesus' teachings and actions is that he demonstrated in his life the very attributes and attitudes toward living that Paul taught later as exemplifying the new age of grace. In other words, Jesus exemplified in his associations and in many of his words a way of life that would later be understood by the first Christians to embody God's way with us in general. Paul taught what Jesus acted out.

Three *Novums*

Jesus taught three entirely new things, three *novums*. First, he taught that his words carried the weight to supersede the words of Moses. This supersession by Christ of the teaching of Moses is displayed consistently in the section of the Sermon on the Mount that is known as the antitheses (Matthew 5:21-48). Here Jesus speaks as follows: "You have heard that it was said to the men of old. . . But I say to you. . . . " The evangelist Matthew is so struck by the extremely sharp contrast that Jesus made between himself and Moses that Matthew prefaces the antitheses by verse 17: "Think *not* that I have come to abolish the law and the prophets." Rather, "not an iota, not a dot, will pass from the law until all is accomplished" (v. 18). The antitheses of Jesus are too hot to handle without a cushioning explanation drawn from somewhere else in the teachings of the Lord. The evangelist thereby waters down the essence of the antitheses. He is reluctant to let them stand alone.

Thus the first *novum* is that Jesus places himself on a par with the Lawgiver — and not just on a par, but in a position that speaks with new and superior wisdom. The historical Jesus radicalized the law by making outward performance and inward intention equivalent. Like Immanuel Kant (1724-1804), who was influenced by the antitheses of the Sermon on the

Mount, Jesus made no distinction between our outward actions and our inward intentions, or the motives behind our actions. Because the will is equal to the deed, and vice versa, no external obedience that is independent of inward desire counts for anything. This explodes the possibility that any external rules or directives can by themselves change the unruly, inward will. According to Jesus, wanting to do the right thing is as important as doing it. Right here, he bursts the borders of his inherited Judaism.

The second *novum* in the teaching of Jesus is his attitude toward the Sabbath, the required day of rest. Here, too, he demonstrates a very different understanding of the law of Moses than that of his contemporaries. In the incident recorded in Mark 2:23-28, the Lord is confronted by Pharisees who criticize his disciples for picking corn to eat on the Sabbath. Jesus speaks with unmistakable clarity: "The sabbath was made for man, not man for the sabbath" (v. 27). That is to say, the good of the human being precedes in importance the command of the law. To put it another way, the requirement of the law is always subservient to the intention that lies behind it. In this case, the precept "do no work on the Sabbath" has come into conflict with the reason the Sabbath was declared in the first place: to provide for the good, in particular the rest and recreation, of humans. Here the striking thing, in addition to the focus on the human being as end in himself/herself from the point of view of God's intention, is the fact that the Lord himself defines what is right and wrong. Jesus defines what is true primordially and therefore what is wrong penultimately. Christ is setting his personal authority over that of Moses, thereby bursting the bounds of his Judaism. His words imply an absolute supersession.

A third *novum* in the teaching of the historical Jesus is his refutation of the laws of purity control. This refutation occurs both in Matthew's Gospel and in Mark's Gospel. Jesus' students are criticized by the Pharisees for not washing their hands before they eat. Christ's answer is adversarial. He contradicts the familiar theory we have already seen of their distinction between the inward and the outward: "Do you not see that whatever goes into the mouth passes into the stomach, and so passes on. But what comes out of the mouth proceeds from the beast, and this defiles a man. For *out of the heart* come evil thoughts, murder, adultery, fornication, theft, false witness, slander. These defile a man; but to eat with unwashed hands does not defile a man" (Matthew 15:17-20; Mark 7:14-23; italics added). The new teaching of Christ consists in his entire focus on the inward being of the person. We are not corrupted by the forces that exist outside us, but by *the* force, sin, that exists within us. Therefore the problem of being human, the problem of struggling with the inward unruly self, is not controlled or resolved by outward correction or amendment. The whole force of the law as a principle for government, both of the self and of the extension of ourselves that is the world, is seen through and thereby drained. The principle underlying the law, the principle of successful amendment of life by means of control, is understood to be totally impotent. The human struggle for control over the will, the self, the "heart," the impulses, the actively aggressive or violating, can never be won on the field of action. No more action! Whatever change must come, must come from within, from the heart of the self.

To sum up, these three *novums* appear in the teaching of Jesus: his explicit personal antitheses to the teachings of Moses; the conception of the human being as an end in himself/herself, or better, as the focal object of the one true Subject, God; and his focus on the inward being and the implacable force of sin within us. Sin lies within the innermost dark continent of human character. In fact, to be a human being is to be a sinner. That is the one fitting and universal description for every human being without exception

Benjamin Clark Cutler (1798-1863), who was an early evangelical in the American Episcopal Church, put well this third insight of Jesus in a sermon preached at St. Ann's Church, Brooklyn, and published in 1857: "Could we see our sins in the light of heaven, they would appear not only numberless, but most criminal and aggravated. Sin would appear in every relation and action of life. . . . Indeed, so universal on this globe has been the breaking of God's law, that our general appellation is that of sinner." Christ's third *novum*, the saying that concerns purity control, deepens and universalizes the problem of being human.

Some of the teachings of Jesus that are collected in the Gospels, especially in the first three Gospels, are intertwined with secondary material and interpretation on the part of the Gospel writers themselves. We know that the process of transmission of Jesus' teaching in its original form to the written form we now possess took a few decades, and perhaps more in certain cases. Moreover, the different editorial intentions, even the different voices of Matthew, Mark, and Luke themselves, not to mention John, who seems to be writing later and with a freer hand, make a big difference in our being able to be certain about what represents the authentic voice of Jesus the teacher.

A familiar criterion by which theologians can know the difference between the editor (i.e., Matthew, Mark, Luke, and John) and the source (i.e., the words of Jesus himself) is the criterion of dissimilarity. According to the criterion of dissimilarity, a saying of the Lord is estimated to be authentic only if it could have been said neither by a Jewish rabbi contemporary with Jesus nor by a Hellenistic or Greek philosophical teacher contemporary with him. Add to this criterion of dissimilarity a third wish that Rudolph Bultmann (1884-1976) and his students expressed, to call inauthentic or secondary any saying of the Lord that might conceivably have been added or added to by the first Christians in the first enthusiasm of their belief that Jesus had risen from the dead.

These three categories of negation or dissimilarity — that is, the Jewish, the Hellenistic-Greek, and the early Christian — are a heavy burden for any New Testament verse to carry. They are the albatross of an overly zealous, we might even say angrily zealous, criticism of the Bible. Even so, each of the three *novums* in Jesus' teaching pass all three tests. They could have been expressed neither by a conforming Jewish rabbi, nor by any Hellenistic Greek thinker anyone knows of, nor by an avid disciple in the exuberance of earliest Easter enthusiasm. The three *novums* we have stated are important, powerful, even shattering insights concerning the Jesus of history in his uniqueness.

The Discontinuity of Jesus

Christian theology is Christology by definition. The teaching of Jesus opened a vein of powerful discontinuity in the history of religion, and certainly within the history of the Bible. Jesus' teaching is discontinuous at its deepest stratum with the inherited Judaism codified by Moses and those who composed the Old Testament in the voice and authority of

Moses. The discontinuity of the figure and teachings of Jesus, the first Christian as we understand him, becomes the prism through which theology is organized and presented. This discontinuity declares a theology of grace in tension with the law, a theology of God and humanity in I-thou conversation. But there is more to the discontinuity of Jesus' teaching as it is reflected in the three *novums*. There is the discontinuity of his life.

In order to appreciate the uniqueness of the historical Jesus, we need to evaluate not his continuity but his discontinuity with Judaism. This is because his discontinuity with the historic biblical faith from which he emerged reveals what is unique and therefore what is universal about his life. Jesus diagnosed the human condition in much more radical terms than traditional Judaism before him, for he saw the inwardness and the totality of human defilement and corruption. He observed the full effects of the Fall. "Jesus felt himself in a position to override, with an unparalleled and sovereign freedom, the words of the Torah and the authority of Moses. This sovereign freedom not merely shakes the very foundations of Judaism and causes his death, but, further, it cuts the ground from under the feet of the ancient world-view with its antithesis of sacred and profane and its demonology."[3]

Thus Jesus also became separated from classical thought, that is, Greco-Roman thought. Greco-Roman thought in general ascribed to the human will far more control, even the ability to detach and separate itself from outward negativity and outward circumstances in general, than Jesus allowed it. The comprehensiveness of Jesus' attack on all external attempts to master the earth's moral environment makes his thinking as incompatible with Aristotle's as it is with Moses the Lawgiver's. It is critical for systematic theology to begin from the discontinuity of the life and teaching of Jesus. This is not to mention the discontinuity of Jesus' death, which comes to the fore in Chapter Two.

3. E. Käsemann, "The Problem of the Historical Jesus," in *Essays on New Testament Themes* (Philadelphia: Fortress Press, 1982), p. 40.

The Friend of Sinners

A further, important discontinuity in the life of Jesus occurs in connection with his associations or relationships with people. He associated himself by intent with the publicans and the tax collectors (Matthew 9:10-11; 11:19; Mark 2:15-16; Luke 5:29-30; 7:34; etc.).

> The Pharisees and their scribes murmured against his disciples, saying, "Why do you eat and drink with tax collectors and sinners?" And Jesus answered them, "Those who are well have no need of a physician, but those who are sick. I have not come to call the righteous, but sinners to repentance." (Luke 5:30-32)

The Lord saw the kingdom of God dawning in the receptive need of the "godless" sinners, thus prefiguring St. Paul's later interpretation that Christ had died, and lived, for the ungodly (Romans 5:6, 8). We know that Jesus gathered around him many who were outside the law, many who were even heedless and indifferent to it. The remembered association of the Lord with Mary Magdalene (Matthew 27:56; Mark 15:40), with Zacchaeus (Luke 19:5), with the unclean woman who had a flow of blood (Matthew 9:20; Mark 5:25; Luke 8:43-44), with the Samaritan woman at the well (John 4:7), with the Gentile centurion (Matthew 8:8), and with Levi, later called Matthew, the tax collector (Mark 2:14) confirms this. The traditions about his life bear the undeniable stamp of these associations. These associations were his primary circle. In fact, his regard for Simon Peter, whose triple denial at the end is a signature over the atrophied human condition to which in Christian theology the kingdom of God comes, is shorthand for all his other associations with sinners.

The tradition of Jesus' association with sinners presented in fact and incident what later New Testament writers would understand as the primary characteristic of God: his grace and undeserved favor. Grace lived out, in the three-year, barrier-breaking life laboratory of Jesus, became the seed for grace as the content of theology. With the three *novums* of Jesus' teaching is linked the *novum* of his invitation to the publicans and tax collectors. Jesus was the friend of sinners.

The Exorcisms of Jesus

A final *novum* from Jesus' life is the fact, recognized by all schools of thought in New Testament scholarship, that he had a reputation for being an exorcist. Jesus drove out demons from possessed persons. These were persons whom we today would probably understand as suffering from schizophrenia and various kinds of dementia. Jesus' everywhere-acknowledged gift of banishing tormenting spirits was received as a mark of the coming of God's reign upon earth. Thus no one in the history of New Testament criticism has been able successfully to argue out or eliminate Luke 11:20 from the canon of the Lord's authentic received words. It is simply too devastating. Moreover, it is blasphemy to the Jews and foolishness to the Greeks:

> Some of them said, "He casts out demons by Be-elzebul, the prince of demons"; . . . But he said, "And if I cast out demons by Be-elzebul, by whom do your sons cast them out? Therefore they shall be your judges. But if it is by the finger of God that I cast out demons, then the kingdom of God has come upon you." (11:15, 19-20)

The historical Jesus was an exorcist. His authority over the demons indicated the presence of God. It is a familiar idea in theology that Jesus preached the kingdom of God and understood his ministry as ushering in the kingdom of God. The character of the kingdom of God, what exactly it was according to history, as well as its timing and relation to the present moment, has had almost as many interpretations as there have been theologians in the Christian church. It is going no further than the text, however, to say that Jesus' exorcisms were taken, by his followers and also by himself, as proof that history was at a turning point on the road to that kingdom. If he taught nothing else, Jesus taught that history was coming to a crisis. History was at the end of its repetitive cycle.

The First Christian

The so-called "first quest" for the historical Jesus refers to the nine-teenth-century attempt to construct an account of his objectives and achievements biographically. The first quest is usually judged to have ended with the publication of Albert Schweitzer's book *The Quest for the Historical Jesus* in 1906. In that book, Schweitzer depicted Jesus as a failed messianic prophet, crying out on his cross in despair at God's failure to answer his prayers. This first quest ended in scepticism and atheism.

A "second quest" for the historical Jesus began in the early 1950s. It dates from a lecture given to theological graduates of Marburg University by Ernst Käsemann on 20 October 1953. The second quest made important progress toward identifying the main marks of Jesus' ministry as he lived it within time and space. Much of the second quest's achievement has been not so much wiped away as forgotten. It has been trampled over in the exuberant *Schadenfreude* of the North American "Jesus Seminar." The Jesus Seminar regards itself as a "third quest" for the historical Jesus.

Here is the principal conclusion from Käsemann's landmark 1954 lecture. It still stands as a powerful achievement in identifying the building blocks of Christian Christology. Käsemann's picture of Jesus is a vital first building block for this short systematic theology.

> The "Amen" [as in, "Truly or *Amen* I say unto you"] of Jesus signifies an extreme and immediate certainty, such as is conveyed by inspiration. Out of this certainty the antitheses of the Sermon on the Mount are pronounced, the Sabbath commandment and the law of purification are assailed; out of it, that dialectical relationship to the Scriptures originates, which is ready to pass by their literal meaning in order to seek in them the will of God; and out of it, the demand for intelligent love is set up and placed in opposition to the demand of the rabbinate for blind obedience. It is by this immediate assurance of knowing and proclaiming the will of God, which in him is combined with the direct and unsophisticated outlook of the teacher of wisdom and perhaps lies behind it, that Jesus is distinguished from the rabbis. It does not matter whether he used the actual words or

not; he must have regarded himself as the instrument of that living Spirit of God, which Judaism expected to be the gift of the End.[4]

Christology, which is the core of systematic theology (**Thesis 1**), begins with the discontinuity of the historical Jesus with the teaching that came before him. This discontinuity pertains to Judaism directly, and less directly to the thought-world of late Hellenistic Greco-Roman thought.

Thesis 2: The historical Jesus was the first Christian. His teachings demonstrate it, his associations embody it, and his exorcisms confirm it.

The Present-Day Christ

The oldest antithesis, or rather, the oldest false antithesis, in New Testament theology is the relation between the historical Jesus and the so-called Christ of faith. The use of these two phrases in relation to one another points to the fact that while Jesus of Nazareth lived within a concrete time and space, the Jesus Christ whom Christians worship is alive today. What is the connection between the historical Jesus and the Christ of faith? This is the second most important question of systematic theology, the first being who was he in lived time? That he was the first Christian we have already affirmed.

The connection between the two entities Jesus of Nazareth and the Christ of faith is the resurrection, the first Easter. By the first Easter we mean the claim that, by a miracle that occurred after his death, the body of the historical Jesus was transformed into a risen, enduring, and also corporeal body who was not destined, like Lazarus who was also raised from the dead, to die again. Christology's claim is that Jesus was raised by God to an ultimate form of existence that is continuous forever after the date of A.D. 29, the year in which Jesus was crucified.

4. Käsemann, "The Problem of the Historical Jesus," p. 42.

1 Corinthians 15:4-8

The most frequently cited passage concerning the resurrection of Jesus is the section of 1 Corinthians 15 in which St. Paul lists Christ's first post-resurrection appearances to his disciples:

> He was buried and was raised on the third day in accordance with the scriptures. He appeared to Cephas, then to the twelve. Then he appeared to more than five hundred brethren at one time, most of whom are still alive, though some have fallen asleep. Then he appeared to James, then to all the apostles. Last of all, as to one untimely born, he appeared also to me. (vv. 4-8)

This is one of the most important texts in the Bible. It indicates that Paul believed that the resurrection of Christ had been witnessed by many. Many of Jesus' followers, who were also Paul's contemporaries, believed that they had seen the Lord — and on at least five different occasions. Verse 8 is particularly important because it says that Jesus appeared to Paul himself. By "one untimely born" Paul refers to the fact that he himself had not known the Lord face to face, nor seen him, nor heard him in the flesh, but that Jesus risen had nevertheless appeared to him. Verse 8 of 1 Corinthians 15 draws us into the territory of personal encounter, for Paul speaks of a supra-historical Jesus. He has himself made the connection between the Jesus of history (there and then) and the Christ of faith (here and now).

Romans 4:24b-25

A second passage that is important for drawing the connection between the two phrases "the Jesus of history" and "the Christ of faith," which have proven so fruitful and also so elusive in the history of modern theology, is Romans 4:24b-25. Here Paul affirms an inseparable connection between the first Easter and the present fruits of it:

God raised Jesus our Lord from the dead, who was put to death for our trespasses and raised for our justification.

The words "put to death for our trespasses" will receive attention later. The point for now is that whatever occurred in the putting to death was confirmed or ratified or "justified" by virtue of the resurrection. The *un*-dead and no-longer-mortal property of the risen Jesus' body makes good the benefits received from his death.

This same insight concerning the resurrection surfaces in a collect (i.e., a set appointed prayer) composed by the English Protestant Reformer Thomas Cranmer for the 1549 Book of Common Prayer:

Almighty Father, which hast given thy only son to die for our sins, and to rise again for our justification; Grant us so to put away the leaven of malice and wickedness, that we may always serve thee in pureness of living and truth. (Collect for the First Sunday of Easter)

The first Easter sets Jesus in the present moment. It is a continuing present.

Thesis 3: The connection between the historical Jesus and the present-day Christ is Easter Day of the year 29.

How is the risen Christ present for us today? The questions just begin.

Where and in what receivable form is the historical Jesus made present in today's moment, a moment in which, according to the Book of Acts, he is no longer present to us according to sight or sound (1:9)? In what way can we have contact with the risen Christ? How does the risen Christ communicate himself to us?

Several possibilities have been offered in response to this question, even from the earliest days of faith. In fact, each of the great living traditions of world Christianity defines theology by the way it understands Christ to be our contemporary. Only one of these ways, however, is able to survive the criticism of reason as we survey the long course of Christian history in regard to Christ's contemporaneity. Moreover, only one of these ways stands up to the reality of pastoral ministry to people as it really works and functions — and as people really work and function! This surviving, effective possibility proves to have the uncomfortable substance of a negation rather than an affirmation — or, better, it proves to be an affirmation that consists of a negation.

Here are some of the theories that have been developed over twenty centuries to try to make concrete, or more precisely, objective, the presence of the risen Christ to the human being.

Theory 1: He is present in the sacraments. This idea is that Christ is present objectively in the "elements" of the eucharist, that is, in the bread and wine, and in the water of baptism.

Bread and Wine

In this development of Christian theology, the blessed bread and wine of the Passover meal, the constituents of Jesus' last supper on earth (Luke 22:7-38), become in some real actuality the place or "temple" of Christ's presence with us now. This becoming is understood by the words "transubstantiation," "consubstantiation," "real presence," or whatever words are descriptive — no words finally can be — of an objective change in the bread and wine by which they become the present location of Christ's body and blood. The concept here, the conviction here, is that Jesus Christ is objectively present in the sacrament of the body and blood.

Water

A certain understanding of baptism, linked to this understanding of the mass or eucharist, takes a similar view of the water that is set aside for the sacrament of Christian initiation. The water is changed objectively through the divine power of the Spirit of the resurrected Jesus, activated by precisely correct words and intentions, into the effective channel for the communication of God's grace on earth. Thus baptized children are regenerated or born again. Theory 1 of the risen Christ's presence now objectifies his presence within the bread and wine of the eucharist and also within the holy water of baptism.

Objectification

What is "objectification" in religion? It is the human attempt to locate a tangible object in the tangible world that carries the intangible universality of the divine, invisible God. From the standpoint of this systematic theology, "objectifying" thinking is equivalent to magical thinking. Thus, for example, voodoo, in which cursed and blessed objects also play a vital role, is a textbook form of objectifying religion. Christianity, like all religions, suffers from such thinking. Yet this is a normal human yearning: to put the inexpressible into expressible form. For Christianity, only the body of Christ during his time in history can be considered the objective manifestation of God.

The biblical proof text for most conceptions of sacramental objectivity occurs in the Gospel of Matthew: "Truly, I say to you, whatever you bind on earth shall be bound in heaven, and whatever you loose on earth shall be loosed in heaven" (18:18). This text, which has been used, on the one hand, to buoy the papacy (in its alternate form, from Matthew 16:19), and, on the other hand, to buoy high theologies of the preached Word of God — not to mention the so-called power of the "keys," that is, the absolving power of the church's priest or minister in relation to private confession — gives authority to the human representatives of Christ on earth to speak for God. Whatever the exact context in which Jesus spoke these words, their meaning inevitably concerns our great question of the objective contemporary intersection of the human and the divine. The question for us is always formulated in this way: How is the risen Christ communicated to the human being who lives after Christ's days in history, the person who lives after the period of Christ's days on earth?

The problem presented by Matthew 18:18 is that it can be applied to almost anything. It can be taken to refer to the pope; to the priesthood or ordained ministry; to the confessional; to the words of consecration at the eucharist or communion; to the preaching of God's Word from the pulpit; to the pentecostal laying on of hands for healing; to the anointing power of the Holy Spirit as expressed in tongues and prophecy; or to any individual's personally held conviction that he or she is speaking for God. In other words, Matthew 18:18 is able to be a free-floating endorsement of the precious intersection between God and humanity. Such an intersection, wherever its true point is to be found, is the indispensable element of a living religion.

It is no wonder that, in connection with the realistic language of blood and flesh that is found in John's Gospel (6:50-59) and backed by the free-floating authority of Matthew 18:18, the Christian church, at least large sections of it, developed an objective theology of the Lord's Supper. It suffices to say here that Matthew 18:18 is a text to which any form of objectification, any attempt at objectification in religion, will be attracted.

Theory 2: **The risen Christ is present in the words of the Bible. This is a second way to objectify the resurrection, and it takes more than one form, each of which has had a large following in the history of Christianity.**

The Written Words

One form of this idea is that the risen Christ is objectively present in the text or *written words* of the Bible; the words of Scripture bear within themselves the objective presence of God. In some church interiors, a Bible is prominently displayed on the altar or communion table or wherever the sight lines converge. This is both symbolic and also more than symbolic. Like the elements of the eucharist kept reserved on Roman Catholic altars, the Bible at the apex of the sight lines becomes the holy tabernacle of God. And like the varying descriptions for the divine presence in the bread and wine, verbal descriptions abound for the precious concretion of the presence of God in the written words: "mechanical inspiration," "entire sufficiency," "verbal inerrancy," "verbal infallibility," and so forth.

Words vs. Word

Some will separate or distinguish the words of God (the text) from the Word of God (the Christ to whom the text points or the Christ whom the text bears). This tactic, which is a tactic of differentiation, takes varying forms, as do all the other theories concerning the objective communicability of the risen Christ. It all depends on the degree to which the theologian of divine presence wishes to be objective and thus to speak in objective terms about the mediating thing. If the characteristic theology of object in Roman Catholicism relates to the elements of the eucharist, the characteristic theology of object in Protestantism relates to the Word of God written. *Both historic streams of objectification, the Roman Catholic and the Protestant, are attempts to receive the resurrection.* They are deeply felt and yearned for attempts to receive, even to capture, the ineffable. They are human attempts to pin down that which cannot be pinned down.

Even the one concrete and universal Christian symbol of the appearance of the grace of God, the cross of Jesus, represents the hiddenness and, from our end, the inaccessibility of God in any objective form. In the cross of Jesus, God operates *sub contrario*, under the opposite of his reasoned attributes such as strength and authority and life. In the cross, which is an objective symbol of Christ's objective life on earth, the symbol belies the reality to which it points. God takes his stand on earth within the human experience of kinked, crooked desperateness.

Countering the Charge of Reductionism

There is a theological strategy or argument by which beliefs concerning the Word of God written as the communicating instrument for the presence of the risen Christ are able to evade the charge of reductionism. The charge is that we reduce the risen Christ to something manageable and therefore limited and bound in some way to human uses and intentions, possibly even something to be controlled, when we claim that he comes to us objectively through the words of Scripture. The charge remains potent even if we disconnect the words of Scripture from the Word of Scripture. The charge remains potent even if we reply that he speaks to us through the Bible as a whole or "in plenary" rather than in mechanical terms. The Bible in plenary can still reduce the communication of God to a book.

An answer to this charge that the Bible in Protestantism can become something reducible to human management is the contention that it is the Holy Spirit of God who invisibly quickens the words and makes them become to us the Word. The same answer is sometimes given in respect to the elements of the eucharist and the water of baptism: the Holy Spirit invisibly makes them become *to us* the great thing they are intended to be. The emphasis then is not on the material thing, such as the book, the water, or the bread and wine. The emphasis is rather on the creative action of God enlivening the book, the water, and the bread and wine. This is the most commonly deployed answer to the criticism of objectification. This answer prevents a one-to-one or instrumental correlation between a given material object and the presence of the risen Christ. For such a one-to-one correlation would be magic! Even the defenders of objectifying thinking allow that it is magic when any object available to be touched in this world is endowed *in itself* with a divine attribute or appellation. No physical object can be impregnated with divinity. Not one. If that were so, then religion would consist entirely and only in finding and possessing the divine object. The ancient search for the Holy Grail, not to mention the Ark of the Covenant, the true wood of the cross, the footprints of Mohammad, Roswell, Noah's Ark, the Bo Tree, the Shroud of Turin — all of these are magical quests.

The problem with this resort to the Holy Spirit is that it cannot be criticized. The presence of the Holy Spirit in connection with an object can neither be proven empirically nor disproven empirically. In fact, there is really nothing we can say to give any account of it at all, apart from personal experience. That is because it is invisible. True, thousands and millions of persons would say with conviction that they have experienced the risen Christ through the words of Scripture become the Word from God by virtue of the power of the Holy Spirit. Likewise, through the elements of bread and wine become the body and blood by that same transformative power, thousands and millions of persons would say with equal conviction that they have experienced the risen Christ. But no account of this can be given. No generally agreed upon statement can be made concerning how, when, and where that would not be magical.

Even the Bible says, *by its own counter argument,* that "the wind [of the Spirit] blows where it wills, and you hear the sound of it, but you do not know whence it comes or whither it goes; so it is with every one who is born of the Spirit." Nicodemus replies, as must we, "How can this be?" (John 3:8-9). Likewise, the woman of Samaria draws powerful words from Jesus in John's Gospel concerning the de-objectification of all religious practice: "Woman, believe me, the hour is coming when neither on this mountain nor in Jerusalem will you worship the Father. . . . But the hour is coming, and now is, when the true worshipers will worship the Father in spirit and truth, for such the Father seeks to worship him. God is spirit, and those who worship him must worship in spirit and truth" (4:21, 23-24).

The Holy Spirit has been the classical point of intersection in theology between *then* (when Jesus lived) and *now* (when we live). The Spirit has also been the classic point of intersection between *there* (where the risen Jesus "is", at "the right hand of the Father") and *here* (where we live). The Holy Spirit is a true fact — better, a true factor in biblical theology. The problem comes when the human being wishes to summon the Spirit on command. This proves impossible. It is impossible in every single case, without exception. God could not allow this, ever, for then he would be ours and not we his.

The fact is that one Sunday's mass may be deeply meaningful to me, the next Sunday's wan and lifeless. One day's Bible study may knock me flat and demolish my complacency, the next day's may leave me cold. It is not quite so capricious within the common experience of Christian people, but the Spirit has never performed on command.

The present-day Christ, the christological center in the present moment of this systematic theology, requires a better account of himself. How can he be received by someone at *any* given point, at any given time? Better, how can he be received always and everywhere? Evangelically — that is, from the standpoint of the *evangelium* or gospel — we are required to give up all ideas of sacred time and sacred space.

Theory 3: The risen Christ is able to be represented concretely in the visual, and in particular through the icon.

This is the next possibility to assess and also to disarm. It is potent within the tradition. Moreover, it is mightily potent within the human heart.

Here, in relation to the icon or sacred painting, we come to a form of Christianity that is of crossover importance in relation to high culture. The appeal of the visual arts to people who hunger and thirst after the "unknown God" (Acts 17:23) has never been more obvious than it is in the decades of "monster" exhibitions of Picasso's work, Van Gogh's, Manet's, Jackson Pollock's, etc. There are many people for whom a picture by Mark Rothko is the closest thing to God they can imagine. In front of St. Thomas Church at 53rd Street and Fifth Avenue in New York City, long lines of people stand for hours every Sunday morning to see special exhibitions of high art at the Museum of Modern Art. They are like the lines of people queuing for ashes on Ash Wednesday or for communion on Christmas Eve. They completely block worshipers of the old God from entering *their* temple, the great Episcopal church in mid-Manhattan that stands next to the museum, in favor of known yet unknown gods like Paul Cezanne and Andy Warhol.

The hopes placed on the visual to represent the divine go back to the earliest history of human beings. Despite Christianity's early negation of the visual, inherited from the second commandment of Judaism, such primordial hopes entered the Christian tradition quite early and peaked in the rise of the icon. The icon or painted image of Christ or a Christian saint is constitutive of the Orthodox tradition within Christianity. By "Orthodox" is meant the Greek Orthodox Church, the Russian Orthodox, the Serbian Orthodox, the Romanian Orthodox, the Armenian Orthodox, and so on. In the faith tradition indicated under the title "Orthodox," the religious painted image is understood to bear the presence of the risen Christ to the believer who views it today.

The Orthodox tradition usually concedes that it is not the icon as such, the wood and the paint, that presents the risen Christ. Rather, it is the Holy Spirit carrying that presence through the inspired image to the believer who views it in faith. When thousands of people fall on their knees to this day at the daily unveilings of the Roman Catholic Church's "Black Madonna" in Çzestochowa, Poland, they are believing that the Holy Spirit opens the "eyes of their hearts" (Ephesians 1:18) to perceive Christ truly as he is present in the icon. It is a powerful experience to be a part of that devotion. It is powerful to be present anywhere near it.

Nevertheless, it is a concept that is hopelessly over-freighted. It cannot possibly deliver what it promises to deliver. It is over-freighted because no tangible object subject to "moth and rust" (Matthew 6:19), deterioration and decay, can bear the weight of such hopes.

The icon is part of a category of beauty that lies in the eye of the beholder. The worshiper may bring to the icon a deeply felt faith, but the icon as the objective bearer of the risen Christ cannot be a possible thing. It could be possible within a given situation through the influence of the Holy Spirit. But we have already seen that the Spirit "blows where it wills" (John 3:8), and no human being exists who can summon it by impulse or by wish. The same is true of the power of any visual image of any type. Its communication is too subjective. One person's Picasso is another person's Bougereau. The power of the image is not stable. Power does not stay or persist with the object. The existence of fashion proves this. Van Gogh could not sell a self-portrait when he was here. Now he would not be able to keep one to himself. The Bible is right to proscribe the worship of images. In doing so, the Bible proscribes our will from subjecting God to the human word of command.

Theory 4: **There is another tradition in Christianity that locates the presence of the risen Christ elsewhere than in the sacraments (i.e., the Catholic strand), the written Word (i.e., the Protestant line), or the visual image (the Orthodox approach). This is the tradition known as Pentecostalism. It is the charismatic or "Holy Spirit" strand.**

This tradition picks up from the New Testament church at Corinth, in which the Christians believed that Christ was risen in the form of ecstatic spiritual gifts given by his Spirit to the congregation (1 Corinthians 12:1-13). These ecstatic spiritual gifts included speaking in unknown languages or tongues; prophetic utterances directly from God; the interpretation in common speech of the unknown tongue-speaking; miraculous, sometimes instantaneous healings of physical disease; etc. The presence of the risen Christ was manifest through and in the gifts as expressed during worship and assembly.

The Pentecostal strand in Christianity is extremely compelling. It is also infectious. If God is really *there,* in the gifts, then we had better get to church, or at least to that church in which the gifts are coming forward. A specific form of the Pentecostal teaching occurs under the heading of "the anointing." This teaching, widespread in African-American Pentecostalism but also reaching far beyond it, focuses on the anointing of a person by the Holy Spirit through the medium of oil. In some influential Pentecostal circles, the anointing is prayed for with one's whole heart, received concretely at the hands of the pastor, and understood as *the* mark of God's work in one's whole life. The anointing becomes as sacramental in the circles within which it is sought as the consecrated Host is in Catholicism or as the written Word is in some forms of Protestantism or as the sacred picture is in Orthodoxy. Pentecostalism is another distinct form of the hunger we have seen all along the spectrum of Christian traditions to locate the presence of the risen Christ within space and time.

As if that were possible!

It is not possible. It is absolutely impossible if we are to take seriously Jesus' words about worshiping God in spirit and in truth (John 4:24), not to mention the prescript that God is uniquely present only where love exists (1 John 4:7-12). Both the Spirit as the unseen Christ and love as the unseen *élan vital* of human experience make it impossible to confine God to any *form.* Objectification is out! God has never existed in form, save during a short period of time from roughly 4 B.C. to A.D. 29. That period is unique, and it cannot be repeated. Would that it could be!

So again, where is the presence of the risen Christ to be found?

Theory 5: A further strategy within the Christian tradition for locating the presence of God in space and time is the *option for the future.* If the risen Christ is satisfactorily or receivably present neither in the bread and wine, nor in the written Word, nor in the visual image, nor in the anointing of the "baptism in the Holy Spirit"; if the risen Christ is not present tangibly in the days after his physical departure, then maybe he is present in the future. He is on his way toward us in such a way that he will arrive, but we do not know when. "People, get ready, there's a train a comin'."

A future-oriented vision of the risen Christ's presence on earth solves the insoluble problem of untenable sacred space. This is because it limits the question to *time.* The question is not where is he present now, but when will he be present then. The option for the future, which builds on the New Testament promises concerning Christ's return, is important and creative theological thinking.

But a postponed answer to the human being who is facing his or her own death equals no answer at all. We still wish to know how Christ can be known today. The future, in a sense, is no good to me — or at least the future of this world in which I come as a short breath and a single heartbeat, alone and destined to die. The future's promise may sustain me for a time, but not for all time. Not for all my time! Promise is too abstract a quantity to sustain human beings for the duration.

This is why future-oriented theology goes well with political revolution. If Christ and his kingdom are coming, definitely but I do not know when, maybe I can speed up the process by setting things in motion. Maybe I can become proleptic, proactive. Maybe I should become a freedom fighter for the people. The future needs a kick-start. The future needs me!

Or, if none of that works in a lasting manner, we have to face the fact, if it is a fact, that we have *nothing tangible and visible, nothing within time and within space,* to go on.

Thesis 4: In looking for the presence of the risen Christ now, we have nothing that is sufficient to withstand the "moth and rust" that corrupt (Matthew 6:19-20) and nothing satisfactory to withstand the objection that *forms* of every kind can be subjected to the tirelessly self-interested human will.

The Presence of His Absence

Theology must grapple with the empirical fact of the non-tangibility of the risen Christ. Theology must grapple with Christ's non-tangibility in the period following the forty days after the resurrection of A.D. 29 (Acts 1:9), which is the 99.99 percentile of human history. The hungered-for interaction of God's kingdom and the present tense comes down to a negation. This negation we term the presence of his absence. It is the iron ration of Christian existence in the here and now. It reflects the "24/7" (i.e., 24 hours a day/7 days a week) setting of the human relationship to God.

The illusory or at best fading tangibilities of sacrament, written Word, visual image, and even future hope as guarantor in the meantime — these hoped-for tangibilities are all at root ways to possess God on human terms. They are all rusted and consumed over time, as well as turned and tilted to suit the convenience of the "natural man" (1 Corinthians 2:14-16).

Christians live, rather, in the presence of his absence. What does it mean to live in the presence of his absence?

We approach here what Dietrich Bonhoeffer (1906-1945) probably intended by the phrase "religionless Christianity," although Bonhoeffer saw this as a new development in the history of the church, whereas it has, in underlying reality, been in the world or with the world since the bodily departure of Jesus on Ascension Day. We are also not too far from what Luther meant by the phrase *deus absconditus,* the hidden or concealed God.

Bonhoeffer saw Christians as needing to live in a new way because modern thinking had "pushed out" or superseded objective ideas about God. The *forms* of religion, for example, the objectifying mediators we have surveyed, cannot withstand the scrutiny and criticism of the "modern." So they need to go. Better, they need to be made penultimate rather than ultimate.

Luther, from his side, demythologized the instruments of human religion by typifying most of them as being forms of a "theology of glory," by which we are blinded to the true reality of God, who is always hidden beneath and within suffering. God is known on earth *sub contrario* — under his opposite. If you want to find the presence of the risen Christ, you can find him paradoxically in loss, despair, suffering, and solitude. For God's glory dwells always in the cross, under the cross, in the form of rejection, termination, and the loss of faith. The iron ration of Christian living consists in the absence of the tangible and the presence of that absence, as in solitude and a continuing state of loss.

This quality of Christ's presence in his absence is captured uniquely in the paintings of Reformed church interiors by the Dutch artist Pieter Saenredam (1597-1665), and in particular in the paintings he created during the final and most important phase of his creative life (1646-1665). Saenredam's treatments of the chancel of St. Bavokerk, Haarlem, painted in 1660, show a medieval church cleansed of every single medievalism, save one striking, moveable piece of liturgical furniture. It is a moveable wooden pulpit. There is no preacher in the pulpit. Christianity has become invisible: no mediator! The painting evokes the spiritual, the "spirit-and-truth" Word of Jesus in John 4:24, the finally fully abstracted character of God's abiding presence with us in the negation of the object. Saenredam's picture is a full symbolic stopping point for the New Testament theology of God's non-tangible presence in the world after Christ's physical departure in the year 29.

Thesis 5: The risen Christ is present in his absence.

The sense of loss that characterizes the Christian life when it is not propped up by objective mediators of the absolute has a distinctive courage to it. It is a standing to adulthood that has something in common with the mood of classic existentialism. It relates to Immanuel Kant's (1724-1804) definition of "Enlightenment" in his 1783 essay entitled "What Is Enlightenment?" Enlightenment, wrote Kant, is the process of growing up and making decisions for yourself rather than allowing other entities to make decisions for you. The loss or sense of aloneness implied by the presence of his absence is a facing of the truth concerning the non-mediated character of our relation to God, which is Christ's risen Presence.

God is therefore always with us and everywhere with us, but not with us now in any particular time or space. Christianity is an orientation of the whole person to the God who is out there and therefore everywhere, yet who has been identified for us by the teachings and life of Jesus. This orientation is the result of both hearing the word of the Second Commandment concerning the exclusively nonrepresentable nature of God and at the same time hearing the story of Jesus, who embodied the news of what God is like in relation to people, the objects of his subjectivity.

Can we say more about the presence of Christ in his absence?

Thesis 6: The presence of Christ's absence is found within the works of love.

There is an unseen presence within the historic absence that is in fact more tangible and more universal than any of the symbolic or objective substitutes we have criticized as being insufficient, unworthy, and autonomous in relation to God's will. There is only one "form" of the unseen presence of his absence that persists in every age and time. The form of his absent presence is the form of love.

John's first epistle offers us the key text to describe the dwelling place of the risen Christ in the present moment. "No one has ever seen God; if we love one another, God abides in us and in love is perfected in us. . . . God is love, and he who abides in love abides in God, and God abides in him" (4:12, 16). The temple of God on earth is the love we have for one another and for him. John links the two, saying that "he who does not love his brother whom he has seen, cannot love God whom he has not seen" (v. 20). God lives in the perceptible moment within the instrument of our love for one another and for him.

This is an idea with a fairly sentimental history in literature. It could appear to reduce the transcendent God to the horizontal relationship of two or more human beings. "All you need is love." Yet the Bible teaches it, referring to Christians as the people who are "rooted and grounded in love" (Ephesians 3:17). The Bible also typifies the horizontal love of person to person by analogy to the vertical love of God to persons: "In this is love, not that we loved God but that he loved us and sent his Son to be the expiation for our sins" (1 John 4:10). The "expiation" aspect comes in the next chapter, but note that love is given a *content* here. The content of love is the particular form of love demonstrated by Christ in his death and life. We can put this in one sentence:

Thesis 7: The absent risen Christ is present in human love where and when such human love resembles his love when he was here.

The presence of the risen Christ in the works of love is consonant with another important theme in theology: the prior relation of grace to works. The Reformers understood St. Paul to be saying in his epistles that the belovedness that is the experience of the grace of God precedes the loving that is the fruit of good works. In the same way that Christ's historic coming to earth precedes the links of love that are his presence in the setting of his absence, the coming of grace into the lives of humans precedes their being able to get outside of themselves and love others in a degree that is disinterested. In other words, "we loved because he first loved us" (1 John 4:19). Belovedness is prior to loving. The historic fact of the divine love prior to the dwelling of Christ after A.D. 29 within the grace-full works of love offered up by people is mirrored in the repeating experience of everyone who has ever found that unselfish acts flow out of being on the receiving end of unselfish love. Belovedness is always prior to loving.

The classic Reformation understanding of the Christian life as being a life of love flowing from the prior experience and consideration of being loved by a graceful God coheres with the conception here. The Reformation understanding of the works of the love proceeding from grace, never the other way around, coheres with the conception that the presence of Christ exists concretely only in the works of love. Those works themselves resemble the graceful form of love that Christ expressed when he lived on earth. The works of love derive from prior grace. The works of love since A.D. 29 are pressed and stamped with the image of Christ's life from 4 B.C. to A.D. 29.

The Expanding Christ

At least two cities in South America have constructed monuments that evoke deep feelings of reassurance and comfort from Christians as they fly over them just before landing. These are the giant statues of Christ that overlook the cities of Cochabamba in Bolivia and Rio de Janeiro in Brazil. The size of these statues alone, not to mention their awesome siting so as to be seen by everyone in the cities over which they stand guard, is a visual demonstration of the Expanding Christ.

While human beings stand alone in terms of the divine accompaniment of the absent risen Christ, they are surrounded at the same time by the magnificent intangibility of the risen Christ. Because he is nowhere in particular, he is everywhere in general. To quote the Prayer Book collect, "we are forever walking in His sight." Moreover, the generality of his presence is not a reversion to the phenomenon that "all cats are grey in the dark." For he is present in the compassionate love of human beings, which mirrors his love for us when he was on earth. His abstraction always becomes concrete in the particular love that is grace. "From his fullness have we all received, grace upon grace" (John 1:16). This means that Christ has expanded, in the presence of his absence, many, many times.

To observe his compassionate, embracing "body language" in the awesome Christs of Latin America is to reflect on the expansion of that love which is the space/time of his presence now. Ever since the Ascension — and in classic terms since the gift of his Spirit at Pentecost, a gift that we cannot pin down in any penultimate or objective form, for love as such is unseen — the risen Christ has been expanding. He has expanded so widely and largely that his presence in the space of his history here (i.e., Jerusalem and Galilee) has become attenuated to almost nothing. It is harder and harder to find evidence in the "Holy Land" of his historic embodiment. Is he on the Mount of Olives overlooking the Holy City or on the Hill of the Multiplication overlooking the Sea of Galilee? Is he in the ruins of the synagogue at Capernaum? A pilgrimage to Christ on Sugar Loaf at Rio conveys the presence of his absence just as much as a visit to the ruins of the Pool of Bethesda in Jerusalem. More of his presence, in fact! This is because he is incorporeal now. He can expand, and has expanded, through countless ways and means and acts and places and times.

Ray Bradbury, the American science-fiction writer, published a short story in 1951 entitled "The Man." The premise of the story is that the risen Christ has expanded to another planet, and to planet upon planet. The main character of "The Man," a rocket ship captain, blasts off from sphere to sphere in an everlasting search for Christ. The captain is a kind of Flying Dutchman. He always just misses him, because Christ was already there earlier within the presence of his absence. Only one member of the crew realizes that he is already there because he has been there, and that his being there was marked by healings and a divine love that is still radiant from the lives of the people there. The captain blasts off yet again at the end of the story, impervious to the evident and obvious presence of Christ's absence.

This is science fiction. But it evokes the expansion of the intangible in contrast to the contraction of the tangible. Orthodox extremists in Israel sometimes carry a placard that reads, "Rome is for Christians. Leave Jerusalem to the Jews." That saying represents the true contraction of the tangible. Christians, even those who believe in the existence of sacred spaces and times, cannot agree with it. Everywhere is the province of the risen Christ, for love is all around.

Thesis 8: The risen Christ expands to reach the frontiers of world and cosmos, geography and time. Because he is, since the Ascension, nowhere in particular, he is, since the Ascension, everywhere in general. But this "in general" is not the generality of the whole creation. It is the generality of every expression of compassionate love.

Christ as Subject

My dear Pyotr Nikolayevich,

I have been in Italy for two years now, and these two years have been very significant, both for my work as a composer and in my personal life.

Last night I had a strange nightmare. I was producing an important opera to be performed in the theatre of my master, the Count. The first act took place in a great park filled with statues, and these were played by nude men made up with white paint, who were obliged to stand for a long time without moving. I too was acting the part of one of these statues, and I knew that were I to move a fearful punishment awaited me, for my lord and master was there in person, watching us. I could feel the cold rising through my feet, and yet I did not move. At last, just as I felt that I had no strength left, I woke up. I was filled with fear, for I knew that this was no dream, but reality itself.

Fond greetings from your poor, abandoned friend,
Pavel Sosnovsky.

(Quoted from Andrey Tarkovsky, *Sculpting in Time*
[New York: Knopf, 1987], p. 211)

Christology is the starting and ending point for Christian theology. St. Paul states this, with no exceptions, in 1 Corinthians 3: "For no other foundation can any one lay than that which is laid, which is Jesus Christ" (v. 11). Christ is therefore the subject of theology in the sense of theology's governing theme.

Christ is also the subject of theology in another sense. He is the subject of theology in that he is the subject of our conversation with God. He is the "I" who speaks to "us" of the human race.

The woman at the well of Samaria heard the most subjective Word from the Lord. After he had taught her concerning the unmediated character of the relation to God, after he had cut the life support from all objective instruments in this relation by saying, "God is spirit, and those who worship him must worship in spirit and truth" (John 4:24), he addressed her as to his own subjectivity as Messiah. He said, "I who speak to you am he" (v. 26). This is the signature for the subjectivity of Christ in the conversation between God and humankind. The subject is Christ, in the direct relation, and the object is we, in the direct relation.

The subjectivity of Christ in theology is expressed in the German language by the noun *Anrede,* which means "address." We, in the past, have been addressed under the form of a historical entity. We are being addressed today in the contemporary situation in the full light of the presence of his absence. On the "one fine day" or "yonder" of theology — in the life after death, which is constituted by the fully restored situation of direct relation — we shall all be addressed, for we will "see him as he is" (1 John 3:2).

In the present tense, the risen Christ addresses us from out of the past. This makes all the more poignant our contemporary solitude. "For the creation waits with eager longing for the revealing of the sons of God . . . because the creation itself will be set free from its bondage to decay and obtain the glorious liberty of the children of God" (Romans 8:19, 21). St. Paul describes the present tense of the absence of Christ's presence as a groaning (vv. 22-23). This is the iron ration of a hunger that was once filled and shall once again be filled.

Human existence involves a longing for what could be and should be, yet is not. Christian existence involves a longing for what has been. It is true to say that Christian existence involves a longing for death because death is the doorway to the unmediated relation. Dietrich Bonhoeffer said this memorably on April 9, 1945, when he was taken from his holding cell to be hanged: "For you it is the end; for me it is only the beginning."

C. S. Lewis created the world of Narnia to depict the object of this Christian longing for the "over there" of God. Thus in *The Last Battle,* he envisaged the door to the next world which from *this* side looks so forbidding but from *that* side seems so insignificant as to be almost forgotten. Thus John Bunyan's *Pilgrim's Progress* is a long and eventful lead-up to its climax: Christian's crossing the Jordan, his drowning beneath its billows, and his reawakening with a burst of celestial light upon the other side. Death is the doorway to the unmediated relation.

Thesis 9: Christ is the subject of theology because he begins the conversation and also because he concludes it. He concludes it in the sense that the final condition of life consists of the unending and also unbroken position of access to him.

John the Revelator portrays this last condition, at the end of the absence of his presence, as follows:

> And I saw the holy city, new Jerusalem, coming down out of heaven from God, prepared as a bride adorned for her husband; and I heard a loud voice from the throne saying, "Behold, the dwelling of God is with men. He will dwell with them . . . for the former things have passed away." (Revelation 21:2-4)

That Christ is the subject of theology, both in the thirty-three years of his historical presence and in the long march and iron ration of his absence since, and also in the final conversation of his unveiled finality that is the Judgment Day, is the beginning and the end of this systematic theology.

Thesis 10: Satan is the second subject of theology.

There is a second conversation partner in the conversation of which Christ is the subject and the human race the object. This second partner makes it a three-way conversation, although his part is played over our heads. The second conversation partner of theology is the devil. The second conversation partner is Satan.

That the human race is subject to powers of wickedness who have personal identity and intention is believed by all the writers of the New Testament without exception. This observation of human subjection to wicked powers begins with the recollected exorcisms performed by Jesus. He spoke often of Satan and Be-elzebul and of the possession they are able to take of the human person (Mark 3:23, 26; Luke 11:18). Jesus saw himself as contending against the devil: "I saw Satan fall like lightning from heaven" (Luke 10:18). He observed Satan creeping at the edge, just beyond the trace, contending even for his chief disciple: "Simon, Simon, behold, Satan demanded to have you, that he might sift you like wheat" (Luke 22:31).

Later, St. Paul thought theologically concerning the human subjection to demons, whom more recent theologians have wished to understand by means of the softened phrase "the demonic." Paul wrote to the Ephesians: "For we wrestle not against flesh and blood, but against principalities, against powers, against the rulers of this present darkness, against spiritual wickedness in high places" (6:12). In the same sense that the divine conversation with humankind is subject to object, and not subject to subject, the satanic conversation with humankind is also subject to object and not subject to subject. The devil seeks always to control and subdue the object. There is not the slightest degree of mutuality in the relation. "Be watchful. Your adversary the devil prowls around like a roaring lion, seeking some one to devour" (1 Peter 5:8).

On the other hand, the conversation between Satan and Christ is between two subjects. This conversation is conducted directly in one place only: in the wilderness. It is adversarial. The outcome is not clear until the end, although theologically speaking it is certain, for the devil's power is only "given from above" (Job 2:1-6). The conversation is related in Matthew's Gospel and Luke's and is referred to in the Gospel of Mark. It consists of three temptations, each of which the Lord rebuffs by means of Scripture. At the end of the temptations Jesus banishes Satan, although Satan returns later in the temporary form of Christ's leading disciple, Simon Peter (Matthew 16:23; Mark 8:33), and also in the form of Christ's betrayer, Judas (Luke 22:3).

We recognize Satan as a subject in three-way relation. He sits at the core of theological reality.

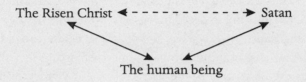

Christians believe that Satan and all the evil demons of the world were overthrown at the cross and stripped of their ability to keep humanity under their thumb. "He disarmed the principalities and powers and made a public example of them, triumphing over them in the cross" (Colossians 2:15). Yet Christians also take seriously the continuing viability of the devil as a seducer, preying behind the scenes on the Achilles heel vulnerabilities of every living person.

Only later, on the other side, yonder, in the establishment of the complete unmediatedness of Christ's presence in heaven, will the powers and principalities be erased forever from existence, "that God may be everything to every one" (1 Corinthians 15:28). Here, now, in the presence of Christ's absence, the devil lives on as a restless predator. He has been overthrown from his high place, but he is a snake in the grass.

This theology underlines the intruding, competitive subjectivity of the devil within the plan of God to subdue the human condition to the good, and moreover the freely chosen good. I wish to affirm the insight of classical Pentecostalism, derived from Pauline language of the New Testament, that the world is a theater of spiritual warfare. Paul sees the human being as an object being fought over by awesome unseen forces. The human being is one who exists at the mercy of the strongest of these powers: Satan or Christ. We wish to see the life, death, and resurrection of Christ as *the* decisive battle for the fate of the race, ending with a victory that constitutes the end and death of the satanic advantage.

Yet this victory, too, like everything else since A.D. 29, is lived out contemporarily in the presence of the risen Christ's absence. It is therefore the more poignant when recrudescent demons strive to get the upper hand within the ambiguity of the present moment. Here we must allow room for a theology of the Holy Spirit. We move to the Spirit's presence within Christ's absence, and in the context of **Thesis 10:** *Satan is the second subject of theology.* Even as he is defeated by the greater Subject, the risen Christ, Satan lives on, in death throes as it were, like the *rigor mortis* of the dying stegosaurus in *King Kong* (1933). Satan's death throes are seismic tremors as far as present individuals are concerned.

How does theology understand Christ's ancient victory over Satan to be effective in the present?

Thesis 11: The Holy Spirit is God's unseen presence operating through the works of compassionate love and in closest relation to Providence.

The Spirit of God

The Holy Spirit is God's presence operating in the absence of the presence of the risen Christ. We have seen that it is an absurd and also a controlling reduction to claim that the Spirit operates, or operates in any automatic manner, within tangible instruments such as the elements of the eucharist, the words of the Bible's Word, the visual image either of sacred pictures or of the pictorial in general, and even the struggle to bring the future's unmediated Presence into the present. We have understood the human being as one who exists in a void. This void is the summary of all circumstances of the human experience, all circumstances of the life that exists on this side of death. Death, however, changes everything.

We have also seen that within the void there is *one* relation or aspect of existence that is eternal. This aspect or relation is the only bridge over from the void to the later unmediated presence of the risen Christ in heaven. This bridge, or bridge experience, is the works of love. It is the works of love that proceed from the belovedness expressed to humankind as object by God as Subject in the unique form of the historical Jesus.

It is the devil's work to frustrate the works of love by entrapping their doers by means of their human weaknesses. Thus the Christian, who lives from belovedness to loving, the Christian who actually does exist through faith for faith (Romans 1:17), continues to exist as if he or she were a character in the theater of spiritual warfare. The devil is alive, and he is also a liar (John 8:44). The human being this side of the new creation is always vulnerable to his suggestion. Therefore the crude theater of control and subjection that characterized human life before the cross is still a layer of human experience after the cross.

Where, then, is the Spirit of God present in that theater of spiritual warfare in the center of which the Christian man and woman stand alone in relation to the absence of the risen Christ?

The Spirit is present in two ways. First, he is present in the love that is grace specifically. Graceful love, the love of unmerited favor, bears the stamp of Jesus' historic love to the tax collectors, publicans, and sinners. It therefore bears the stamp of God's intention toward the world. This was hidden until the coming of Christ. So the Spirit of God dwells in the works of love. They are unconquerable rebukes to sin and the devil. This is the same principle by which Sidney Carton, in the last measure of *A Tale of Two Cities,* did "a far, far better thing . . . than I have ever done before": his sacrifice of grace for the one he loved, and now disinterestedly. The powers of the devil, represented by a political revolution gone mad, are in the case of Sidney Carton's overwhelming sacrifice quelled and overturned. The works of love, which were termed by Luther the "new obedience" or *nova oboedentia,* are the embodied antidote to our experience of Satan.

Second, the Spirit of God is present within the world theater of spiritual warfare in the unseen actions of Providence. Providence, or the oversight of all things by the only autonomous God, is the way God directs the cosmos, and us in particular. Providence is inscrutable, for "who has known the mind of the Lord? or who has been his counselor? . . . How unsearchable are his judgments and how inscrutable his ways!" (Romans 11:34, 33). Nevertheless, God's Providence governs the world and has Satan under restraint. Under attack within the acts of the life's play in which we all play contingent parts, we are able to call upon the Author.

The metaphor of God as Author and us as characters whom he has created has a long history in literature, right down to Stephen King's unnerving little masterpiece *Umney's Last Case* (1993). Unlike these depictions, we, the innumerable characters in search of our Author, are enabled to call upon an Author who has demonstrated the deepest benign disposition in the historical person of Jesus. We are not pleading to a god who underneath a plurality of masks as we experience life is actually a grinning death's head. We are pleading to the one singular autonomous Being who has expressed himself in and as unmerited favor: grace. So we plead the sovereign, defined God in the midst of the devil's seduction as we pursue the works of love. Christians carry the shield of God's Providence, which, while inscrutable in the particulars, is finally and authoritatively governed by the Spirit we have seen in the Man for Others.

Summary

This entire systematic theology develops from eleven theses, restated here:

Thesis 1: Theology is Christology.

Thesis 2: The historical Jesus was the first Christian.

Thesis 3: The link between the historical Jesus and the present-day Christ is Easter Day A.D. 29: the resurrection.

Thesis 4: In looking for the presence of the risen Christ now, we have been given nothing tangible that is sufficient to withstand the "moth and rust" that corrupt (Matthew 6:19-20) or to withstand the inherent tendency to subject all "objectifications" of the divine to our own wills.

Thesis 5: The risen Christ is present in the world by virtue of his absence.

Thesis 6: The presence of Christ's absence is found in the works of love.

Thesis 7: The absent risen Christ is present in human love that resembles his love when he lived here.

Thesis 8: The risen Christ has expanded to reach the frontiers of all human experience. Because he is nowhere in particular, he is everywhere in general. But this is not the generality of our createdness, but the potential universal reach of the works of love that are characterized by grace.

Thesis 9: The risen Christ is the subject of theology, as the human being is the object. The risen Christ is the originator of all conversation between God and the contemporary man and woman.

Thesis 10: The devil is the second, inferior subject of theology.

Thesis 11: The Holy Spirit is the presence of the risen Christ operating through the works of grace and in subjection to Providence.

The starting point for this theology is Christology. Who was Jesus of Nazareth and who is the present-day Christ? We understand the character of the historical Jesus to be the only known predicate or qualifier of the unknown God. Thus we take Harnack's premise as our own: "The Church must take up its position within the system of Christian doctrine where faith takes it, namely, beside the person of Christ, as luminously presented in the Gospels, and witnessed to by His first disciples."[5]

We also understand Jesus to have existed in continuity with the risen Christ. But he is no longer present in the tangible world. He is present neither in sacrament, nor in the words of the Bible, nor in the visual image, nor within his present potential presence arising from the future hope. He is present, rather and only, in the works of love, in the fruit from the belovedness that the gospel story engenders when it grasps us. This love, through which the risen Christ is present, has the character of grace, or unmerited favor. Such loving is the present tense of God's kingdom on earth.

The devil or Satan also exists. He is by his nature seeking to undermine the enactors of the works of love. The devil is resisted by the presence of the risen Christ in the form of sacrificial loving, the works of love that constitute the kingdom of God on earth. The devil is also resisted by the Providence of God.

5. Von Harnack, *History of Dogma*, vol. 7, p. 248.

Systematic theology at this stage of its unfolding is at its christological foundation and core a theology of the providential victory of the people of God who exist to do the works of love within the short band of their human lives.

Yet deep darkness still covers the earth. Not just the devil but also sin and death are enormously powerful, in fact universal entities. There is also the law, which always mediates itself to us in such a way that it negates. *Lex semper accusat* (the law always condemns). The law, theologically speaking, is judicial rather than legislative. If God's subjectivity is superior to Satan's, how has his subjectivity proven superior to sin, death, and the law, which are also our adversaries? He saves us from Satan by the power of the works of love and in the demonstration of Providence. How does he save us concretely from sin, death, and the law? We move now to the content of systematic theology, the power in the blood.

CHAPTER TWO

The Content of Theology:
Power in the Blood

E.F. goes into the audience and picks up a little BABY BOY out of the arms of one of his parishioners. The WOMAN is Vietnamese, as is her baby. Holding the child's tiny hand up in his —

E.F. (APOSTLE) *(continuing):* Look at these beautiful, beautiful little hands; now try to imagine a nail, piercing the palms of this child's hands and then picture the nail going into an old board. I know I don't have enough love in my heart to do this to my son, do you? I know I know I don't! I don't have that much love in me, but God does, God does. *(as he hands the baby back, he says)* Bless you.

> *The Apostle: A Screenplay by Robert Duvall,* 1997, p. 124

For Christ also died for sins once for all, the righteous for the unrighteous, that he might bring us to God.

> 1 Peter 3:18

Wouldn't it be good to be in your shoes
Even if it was just for one day

And wouldn't it be good if we could wish ourselves away
Wouldn't it be good to be on your side
The grass is always greener over there
And wouldn't it be good if we could live without a care.

"Wouldn't it be good,"
pop single by Nik Kershaw, 1984

He who did not spare his own Son but gave him up for us all, will
he not also give us all things with him?

Romans 8:32

Thesis 12: The governing content of Christian theology is atonement.

That "Christ Jesus died for our sins according to the Scriptures" (1 Corinthians 15:3) is the first word in the testimony about Jesus that St. Paul received from the earliest circle of disciples. It is the beginning of the first interpretations of Jesus' death. It is the single most frequently used lens through which Christians in the New Testament sought to understand Jesus. It is also the most profound and most visceral way to understand him. Christ's dying for our sins is the starting point for all further reflection about him, such as the incarnation and the Trinity. No other persisting predicates concerning Jesus can be put to him, no other ontological statements can be made about him, until this first word is understood and valued.

Atonement is the cornerstone of all theology, being the "stone that the builders rejected" which has now become the cornerstone (Matthew 21:42; Mark 12:10; Luke 20:17; Acts 4:11; 1 Peter 2:7; quoting Psalm 118:22). The New Testament writers without exception understood the death of Christ as the fulcrum for all theology because it was the worst thing that could have happened become the best thing that could have happened. The New Testament writers deduced varying themes from this first most important theme, but none of them failed to represent it, even if it is just "lip-service" (as in 2 Peter 1:9, for example), as being the primary, prior affirmation of all. The content of theology is the power in the blood. It is the hub, made indefectibly strong by Christ's resurrection, from which all the spokes of theology derive.

Thesis 13: Christ died for *our sins*.

I slept a little as the day began to lighten — two hours, I guess, maybe three; and I slept the way I always sleep these days in Georgia Pines and hardly ever did then, in thin little licks. What I went to sleep thinking about was the churches of my youth. The names changed, depending on the whims of my mother and her sisters, but they were all really the same, all The First Backwoods Church of Praise Jesus, The Lord Is Mighty. In the shadow of those blunt, square steeples, the concept of atonement came up as regularly as the toll of the bell which called the faithful to worship. Only God could forgive sins, could and did, washing them away in the agonal blood of His crucified Son, but that did not change the responsibility of His children to atone for those sins (and even their simple errors of judgement) whenever possible. Atonement was powerful; it was the lock on the door you closed against the past.[1]

The Christian story of atonement begins with the empirically verifiable fact of original sin. This factor in theological thinking concerning the death of Christ is vital if the atonement is to mean anything.

The old story is true, about the senior seminarian sitting for his ordination exams and being asked the question, "Comment on transactional analysis. Comment on the book *I'm OK, You're OK*." The student thought hard, then drew a little cartoon with a stick figure of Christ on the cross. He pencilled in the following caption: "If I'm OK and you're OK, then

---

1. Stephen King, *The Green Mile* (New York and London: Pocket Books, 1996), pp. 70-71.

what am I doing up here?" The student failed, but in the broader view he passed with flying colors.

The atonement, which implies a required reconciliation of the human being with God, begins from the observation that the individual, and all aggregates of individuals, are impaired intrinsically because of the psycho-genetic characteristic of sin. Sin, therefore, is not an action. This is because sins, sinful actions, spring from sin. Original sin is a part of the constitution of everyone who has ever been born, save the first Adam and Eve before the fall, and the second Adam, Jesus Christ. The myth of Adam and Eve is a true and entirely accurate depiction in story form of the condition in which we find ourselves: creatures in bondage to sin (i.e., the universal defect of nature), the law (i.e., God's just judgment upon the sins that arise from sin), and death (i.e., the universal judgment upon all, all men and women, who cannot exist in the unmediated presence of God, to die).

Dr. Frank Lake (1914-1982), the English psychiatrist known for his eclectic combination of Bible ideas and unorthodox psychological treatments, said an important thing when he was asked at a Church of England ordinands' conference, "Have you ever met someone who was *not* neurotic?" "No," Dr. Lake replied, "but I have heard that there was one once."

The empirically verifiable fact of human fallenness or original sin can be demonstrated with piercing accuracy, not to mention terror, by the history of any given time period and any given sector of the world. "Let your fingers do the walking" through any history book of the twentieth century: from the Armenian holocaust before World War I, through that "Great War," through the Siberian prison camps under Stalin, to the extermination camps under Hitler, to the Cambodian holocaust of the 1970s, to the Rwandan holocaust of the 1990s.

Visit the unevangelized dark continents of any human heart at any time and place. Assess your dreams. Just tell your dreams! Original sin, which means endemic sin, is not the only truth concerning all people. There is also a hunger for grace in all people and a native responsiveness, in almost everyone, to graceful loving. Nevertheless, original sin is one truth, for certain, that concerns every single person.

What exactly is sin? Observing that the human race bears the primordial stamp of a chemistry gone very deeply wrong, what is it, this deep and evenly distributed human proclivity for death and domination? Sin is described conventionally as rebellion against God or the self curved in upon itself or selfishness and self-serving (as opposed to serving the other) or the will to power or missing the mark (for St. Paul, "falling short" of the glory of God — Romans 3:23) or godlessness or unrighteousness or the death wish or libidinal aggression or heedless autonomy, and so on and on.

I would tend to root the definition of sin within the human experience in infancy of fragile dependence, which gives rise to anxiety and trustlessness, which in turn engenders a compulsion to control and subdue. Sin is a chain reaction traveling very rapidly from fear to control. Sin results in frustration, on the one hand, and murderous sexualized aggression, on the other. All these are verbal attempts to capture the immeasurably deep phenomenon of human self-interestedness.

One thing is sure: deep reservoirs of the capacity and potential for domineering and criminal behavior can be observed in everyone. This has caused the history of the world to be a never-ending march of holocaust and conflict, not to mention personal tragedy. When the long-serving Episcopal Bishop of Washington, Angus Dun, was quoted as having said just before he died, "Life is tragic," he was giving voice to an insight that is less disturbing than it is concessive.

"Christ died for *our sins*" refers to the fact that we have all got the problem in common.

We ought to consider the word "self-justification" as a proper description of sin. Sin is self-justification because it argues from *possession*. It argues from the belief that you and I possess an intrinsic differentiation from the other — from God and also from our neighbor. Self-justification implies the individual's holding on to his or her own particular differentiated territory of independent, self-possessed, or contained being. A world village of independent selves is a community of protectionists and defended-lines-in-the-sand sovereignties. The Bible says, in the words of St. Paul, "I have applied all this to myself . . . for your benefit, brethren, that you may learn by us to live according to scripture, *that none of you may be puffed up in favor of one against another. For who sees anything different in you? What have you that you did not receive?"* (1 Corinthians 4:6-7). In other words, all true self-differentiation, all individual identity, is a gift by which the self is freed from the self by means of a different measure, God's measure of grace.

Self-justification is the action of securing and defending one's intrinsic worth. It separates the whole world into as many armed camps as there are human beings. It is the definition of sin, the effects of which are "idolatry, sorcery, enmity, strife, jealousy, anger, selfishness, dissension, party spirit, envy, drunkenness," and the beat goes on (Galatians 5:19-21). Sin as self-justification — the phrase does not exhaust the reality — is a phrase of origin for sins. They are *our sins* because we all drink from the well of original sin.

Thesis 14: Christit died *for* our sins.

The First Epistle of St. Peter brings into relief the *substitutionary* character of Christ's death. This substitutionary character of the atonement needs to be underlined as forcefully as possible: "Christ also died for sins once for all, the righteous for the unrighteous, that he might bring us to God" (3:18). The theme of substitution, of the "for-ness" of the atonement, is set out further in three earliest texts of the Christian era: in Paul's Letter to the Galatians, in his Letter to the Romans, and in his Second Letter to the Corinthians. Thus "Christ redeemed us from the curse of the law, having become a curse for us" (Galatians 3:13); and "sending his own Son in the likeness of sinful flesh and for sin, he condemned sin in the flesh, in order that the just requirement of the law might be fulfilled in us" (Romans 8:3-4); and "For our sake he made him to be sin who knew no sin, so that in him we might become the righteousness of God" (2 Corinthians 5:21).

Sometimes in theology, the "for-ness" of the concept "Christ died for our sins" is softened. It is softened to mean "representation." That is, Christ in his death represented the human race before God. He stood in for the human race in some broadly vicarious sense. The sticking point, however, is the notion of one-for-one, "Christ-for-me" substitution. The sticking point is the "for me" *(pro me)*. The sticking point is the transfer of guilt. "Representation" fails to do full justice to the need for a one-to-one transfer of moral guilt.

The New Testament interprets the death of Christ as a guilt-transfer, according to which the sins and sin of all human beings are counted as Christ's — within the moment of time of his death on the cross. At that moment Christ's sinlessness is counted to all human beings.

There are two main ideas at work here: (1) that it is possible for guilt to be transferred substantially, in its entirety, from one being to another, specifically from one guilty being to another who is innocent and without fault; and (2) that such a transfer occurred within time and space, and in fact at the particular moment when Jesus died (John 19:30 and Luke 23:46-49).

The first idea encounters resistance in some people because it implies the taking away of moral responsibility for sins from the one who has committed them. If such a transfer is envisaged, then such a transfer is obviously unfair. Moreover, it sounds deleterious to moral striving.

It is *not* unfair, however, because Christians see Christ as undertaking the transfer in freedom. He desired to do it. "No one takes [my life] from me, but I lay it down of my own accord. I have power [i.e., the choice] to lay it down" (John 10:18). Christ chose to effect the transfer.

Second, the result of such a transfer is not immorality, which would be taking advantage of the transfer for the sake of further sin, but, rather, thanksgiving for the transfer. St. Paul takes pains to counter the charge that atonement creates a situation of moral laxity or permissiveness (Romans 3:31; 6:1). Paul understands the atonement, the blood of Christ, as enhancing moral existence by virtue of engendering thanksgiving for the transfer (Romans 7:25). The transfer of guilt from one being to another is great good news, concretely for the guilty. And if this be the divine intent, and if he be the principal actor, certainly the burden-bearer of the transaction, then we are freed not arbitrarily nor with the bitter fate on our conscience of the one who really did submit to the yoke of the transfer. Rather, we are calling out for "a thousand tongues to sing" (Charles Wesley)!

Human guilt-transfer is analogous to the divine guilt-transfer, as when an innocent party voluntarily takes the punishment due a guilty one. But the human transfer is not divine. While it may be beautiful and affecting to the emotions, it does indeed raise unanswerable questions ethically — *horizontally*. The *vertical* assumption of guilt that is constituted by the blood of Christ is, on the other hand, a decree from way over our heads. It is also a free decree.

That such a transfer occurred in time and space reflects the emphasis that systematic theology places on the uniqueness of Jesus' historical activity from 4 B.C. to A.D. 29. His activities consisted of unrepeatable events that have reference to the final and ultimate state of things. They were decisive in themselves. We place, admittedly, a very heavy weight on what the Book of Common Prayer, in Cranmer's wording of 1549, calls "the one, full, perfect and sufficient sacrifice, satisfaction, and oblation for the sins of the whole world." But this remains the Christian understanding: the achievement of Jesus in effecting the guilt transfer was a once-and-for-all act. It requires no repetition. Yes, we do tax horizontal historical time, but in the interest solely of understanding the atonement as applying to everyone in his or her present and contemporary moment.

It is necessary to underscore with crystal clarity that the content of theology is the substitutionary atonement of Christ. Theories other than the substitutionary theory, such as the exemplary (i.e., the "liberal") or the "Christus-Victor" (which enhances and does not detract from the substitutionary view), or softer, "lite" views of the cross (i.e., such as "representation") that cover it in velvet, smooth over its angularity, and evade its unbearable confrontation with human sin, fail to do justice to the intensity of the human consciousness of sin.

The human being needs a substitute. This is certainly true in life. Why should not experience inform theology here? We could illustrate the deep spell of the substitution-hope by asking almost anyone, "Would you not like to be somebody else?" Would you not like to be richer, handsomer, prettier, smarter, more self-assured, less insecure, more famous, more successful, happier than you are? Have you never wanted to be someone else's wife or someone else's husband or daughter or son or mother or father? When you look in the mirror, would you not rather have looking back at you someone else's face: the fairest of them all *(Snow White)?* There is not a person alive who at some point or other has not cried out within himself or herself for a substitute. Especially when one faces death!

Logan's Run, an idea-driven science-fiction novel (1967) that was made into a less successful movie (1976) and an even less successful television series (1977-78), makes personal within a fantasy story the universal human need for an individual substitute. Everyone in the overpopulated society within which *Logan's Run* takes place is scheduled to die at age 30, on the dot. No one does not try to escape this fate. No one does not visit the "New You" shop in hopes of prolonging his or her youth. No one is resigned to his or her fate. *Logan's Run* is a parable of the nonnegotiable plea for a personal substitute at the point of death. It describes the way we are made. We crave a substitute in respect to our moral blotter and we demand a substitute in respect to our death. One has been given, and one only. Everything hangs on the One.

Thesis 15: The "for-ness" of God in regard to the human race is prior in theology to the "with-ness" of God.

The "for-ness" of Christ's atonement needs to be set alongside another important, but subordinate, insight concerning his death: its "with-ness." This important but subordinate insight is that Christ died with us. His death is an incarnational point of solidarity with the individual human being, and with human beings in the aggregate, in that he suffers with us in our dying and dies with us in our death. This empathetic and support-ive insight offers strength to the forlorn and to all who suffer in solitude. It is a feature of the atonement insofar as his intention to achieve some-thing for us, the substitutionary conquest of guilt and punitive death, im-plies the parallel intention of embodiment: to exist, albeit for thirty-three years only, alongside and *with* us.

In the context of systematic theology, however, the with-ness of Christ recedes a little in emphasis when compared to his for-ness. It can

59

be observed in its insufficiency to cut the Gordian knot of human loss and pain as well as of human sin by the following true incident from pastoral care. A sincerely intentioned and caring clergyman raced to the home of a couple whose eight-year-old daughter had died of leukemia. He strode into the sitting room, knelt by the side of the grieving father, took the man's hands in his, and looked him in the eyes. He said, "Bill, I just want you to know, I'm here and I care." The father looked up for a moment, with recognition. Then his face darkened. "Frankly, John," he replied, "I don't care that you're here and you care. I want my daughter back!" Empathy and with-ness, no matter how sincere, was not enough. The father wanted a substitute. He wanted a substitute for his daughter lying dead in the bed. He wanted a live daughter in place of his dead one.

The problem of being human consists in the engagement with two life-long irreducible enemies: sin and death. In the case of each confrontation, that with our sin and that with our death, the human being is hopelessly outnumbered, hopelessly outmaneuvered, and hopelessly outgunned. Nothing ameliorative will do. It is an either-or situation: either sin or innocence, either death or life. For everyone living in the world, everyone living for oneself and without God, the end is always the same: regretful death. What is required by God is innocent life. Thus the crucial nature of the substitution: Christ died for our sins, the righteous for the unrighteous, that he might bring us to God.

Thesis 16: Christ *died* for our sins.

Nor was it to offer himself repeatedly, as the high priest enters the Holy Place yearly with blood not his own; for then he would have had to suffer repeatedly since the foundation of the world. But as it is, he has appeared once for all at the end of the age to put away sin by the sacrifice of himself. (Hebrews 9:25-26)

Without the shedding of blood there is no forgiveness of sins. (Hebrews 9:22)

"The blood is the life, Mr. Renfield. The blood is the life." (*Dracula,* 1931 film version)

The "Old, Old Story" of Christ, his making satisfaction for the sins of the world, requires the image — better, the mechanism — of substitution. The human cry to be somebody else is the argument from analogy. We *know* that the self we are exists under judgment. This is experienced existentially in as many ways as there are people. If only we were another! If only we could become another! If only another could substitute for us in our worst nightmare — the moment that we have feared and that has finally come to pass (Job 3:25)! If only another could substitute for us at the moment of our death! The human cry for substitution reflects the biblical fact: God is of "purer eyes than to behold iniquity" (Habakkuk 1:13). We cannot exist in any imaginable quality of proximity to the perfectly pure God. We require a substitute.

Two Metaphors for Substitution

The substitution functions or operates by means of a death for a life. Christ dies in our place so that we can live in his. The substitution in its function, in its instrumentality, can be explained from two metaphors. Neither of these metaphors, however, contains the concept. It is beyond words to contain. It is finally beyond capture.

The Blood

The first metaphor, which in this case is also a living fact, relates to blood. The Old Testament, and ancient culture in general, conceived that the life-principle of every human being, and also of every animal, lay in its blood. When the blood was drained, as in the butchering of animals for sacrifice as well as for food, the life departed. This was empirically obvious. The blood was the life. "For the life of the flesh is in the blood; and I have given it for you upon the altar to make atonement for your souls; for it is the blood that makes atonement, by reason of the life" (Leviticus

17:11). Magic through the ages has picked up on this principle. Voodoo and other magical pathways to control emphasize the power, for ill and also for good, of a creature's blood. The blood carries life, and, more importantly for magic, the blood transfers life.

When the angel smote the Egyptians' first-born in Exodus 12, the angel *passed over* the homes of the Jews. This was because the Jews had daubed the blood of a lamb on the doorposts of their houses. The angel of death accepted, as it were, the blood of the lamb as sacrifice enough. The angel of death accepted the blood as the sign of a rightly sacrificing heart — and specifically in that situation, of the Israelite heart. In the case of the Egyptians, however, who did not know to paint the blood of a lamb over the entrance to their houses, the angel of death was not satisfied until he had taken the life of all the firstborn males.

Blood is the symbol, and more than this, the actuality, of life. The virtue of blood has always been recognized in ritual sacrifice. The blood-spattered mercy seat in the Old Testament religion represented the expiation of God, life for life. It therefore came to represent in Christianity the freedom of the sinner from judgment. Thus William Cowper's hymn of 1779, notorious within modernity for its graphic and literal language, still resonates for every generation. The text never fails to touch the nerve of guilt crying for purgation:

> There is a fountain fill'd with blood
> > Drawn from Emmanuel's veins;
> And sinners, plung'd beneath that flood,
> > Lose all their guilty stains.

> The dying Thief rejoic'd to see
> > That fountain in his day;
> And there have I, as vile as he,
> > Wash'd all my sins away.

The dying of Christ is portrayed in its deepest colors by means of the metaphor and fact of the blood. "There is power in the blood."

The same metaphor is developed in the seventh chapter of Revelation. There the Christians are depicted in a vision as having been purged or "washed" by means of the lifeblood of the Substitute.

> Then one of the elders addressed me, saying, "Who are these, clothed in white robes, and whence have they come?" I said to him, "Sir, you know." And he said to me, "These are they who have come out of the great tribulation; they have washed their robes and made them white in the blood of the Lamb." (7:13-14)

The image is vivid and also startling, because the robes of the people (i.e., their moral standing) have become *white* from being "washed" in *red* blood. This is a strange metaphor, for redness here creates whiteness, and therefore the more abstract meaning about purity is merged with the concrete question in view, cleansing. This is the New Testament version, in visionary, fantastic terms, of the more literal image from the Old Testament:

> "Then you shall take part of the blood that is on the altar, and of the anointing oil, and sprinkle it upon Aaron and his garments, and upon his sons and his sons' garments with him; and he and his garments shall be holy, and his sons and his sons' garments with him." (Exodus 29:21)

The argument of the expression "Christ *died* for our sins" is the affirmation that his blood attaches itself to us as we attach ourselves to him, and the blood gives us purity, indefectible purity. This is one meaning of the repeated service of holy communion. The communion service interprets the historic blood of "the man who died a criminal's death" (Bob Dylan) as being "for all," to all, applicable to all, accessible to all, required by all.

The Courtroom

The second governing metaphor that Christian theology uses to specify and explain the death of Christ — the requirement of his death — is the image of the courtroom. This metaphor is sometimes called the penal or forensic representation of the substitutionary atonement. The idea is often ascribed to St. Paul and his conception of the law, specifically the Jewish law, but beyond that the principle of law and conscience generally (Romans 2:12-16). But the idea of penal or forensic atonement is found in principle throughout the New Testament.[2] It is strong in Augustine, Anselm of Canterbury, Philipp Melanchthon and Reformation orthodoxy, and in almost all species of eighteenth-, nineteenth-, and twentieth-century Protestant evangelicalism.

The metaphor of personal substitution in a court of law speaks to the primal human experience of being caught, and then judged, for a crime. The inner reach of feelings of culpability is so long that one can experience them whether the act at which one is apprehended is itself intrinsically culpable or not. The motion-picture director Alfred Hitchcock never tired of telling the following story from his childhood, a story that he said colored his understanding of crime and punishment forever after:

> *François Truffaut:* Mr. Hitchcock, . . . the only thing I know about your childhood is the incident at the police station. Is that a true story?
> *Alfred Hitchcock:* Yes, it is. I must have been about four or five years old. My father sent me to the police station with a note. The chief of police read it and locked me in a cell for five or ten minutes, saying, "This is what we do to naughty boys."
> *F.T.:* Why were you being punished?
> *A.H.:* I haven't the faintest idea. As a matter of fact, my father used to call me his "little lamb without spot." I truly cannot imagine what it was I did.[3]

In 1954 "Hitch" made a film entitled *The Wrong Man,* in which he developed the idea of a guilt-transfer, a specific substitution of guilt for innocence and innocence for guilt, within explicit Christian images and symbols.

Penal or forensic substitution envisages a law court in which a person is found guilty of a capital crime. The defendant is sentenced to death.

---

2. See James Denney's unsurpassed chapters 2-5 on the atonement in the New Testament in *The Death of Christ* (London: Tyndale, 1951), pp. 41-55.

3. François Truffaut, *Hitchcock* (New York: Simon and Schuster, 1967), p. 17.

Then, to the astonishment of everyone, the judge asserts that he himself will descend from the judgment seat and take the place, through a conscious choice, of the one over whom he has just pronounced the capital sentence. The innocent judge goes on to die in the place of the guilty criminal. Words cannot capture the power of this vivid image. It is the First Peter text come to life, the image of the Just giving his life for the unjust.

Objections

Some would object that the idea of penal substitution is inherently unjust, but this objection misses the point. There is a reversal of roles, a reversal of actual moral responsibility, which only God can undertake. God is free. God is free by definition to undertake such a reversal. "Behold the Lamb of God, who takes away the sin of the world" (John 1:29, 36). God is free to do this. He is the only Being who is both free and able to effect moral transfer (John 10:18).

A second objection to the courtroom metaphor of penal substitution regards its capital or life-and-death intensity. The stakes could not be higher. Yet we must underline the life-and-death character of the guilt transfer. The Bible says that the wages of sin is death (Romans 6:23). This means that the judgment of God is capital. That is not too extreme a statement of the case. If you were to take the sum of any one person's life — her or his thoughts, conscious and unconscious; the dreams, both day dreams and night dreams; the sum of his or her concrete actions, both covert and open to public scrutiny; the motives and intentions; the "body language" — if you were to take the whole sum of a person's life and show it to that person within a moment in time, the person would have a heart attack or a stroke, right on the spot. There are no exceptions to this postulate, certainly not in the Bible. Our inner fears of exposure confirm it absolutely.

Confirmation from Pastoral Experience

As a parish minister, whenever I say this, whenever I state the capital character of the judgment on human sin — inscribed within our own perceptions of reality, not to mention declared in the Bible — I get no argument.

Most people know it instinctively. They remember certain experiences they have had that almost no one else knows about. They know "what dreams may come" (Shakespeare and Richard Matheson). They know the overwhelming waves of hostility and aggression that sweep over them, often in situations when another person standing right next to them has not the slightest idea of what they are really thinking. Did you know there is a Vesuvius standing, smiling and calm, all hearts and flowers, just three feet away from you?

In systematic theology, this particular argument, this confirmation from experience concerning the life-and-death character of Christ's personal substitution for our guilty selves could be regarded as irrelevant, for it is an argument from *life!* It is not proof from the logic of thought. Nevertheless it is fair play, even within the context of classic systematic theology. Luther himself said: *non est speculatio aut meditatio de theologia, sed sensus et ipsa vis theologiae.*[4] This can be translated: "It is not speculation or meditation that we should derive from theology, but rather experience and our very own strength to live." With excellent precedent — the best precedent being the Epistles of St. Paul — we can distance ourselves from an approach to systematic theology that rules out experience in favor of conceptual thinking solely. It is the interplay of concept and pastoral experience that gives to systematic theology its claim to be biblical, not to mention empirically verifiable. The one level where biblical theology stands empirically verifiable is the ground-floor level of original sin.

Substitution in Literature

We can take a further step, however. Pastoral experience and clinical observation bear out the very gripping fear of exposure that people with every sort of exterior and personal history carry. But important examples of art and literature carry the same theme, the same threat, of capital judgment in the transfer of guilt.

4. From a letter to Nicholas van Amsdorf dated November 25, 1538. See Gerhard Ebeling's summation of Luther's theological thought in its relation to pastoral care, *Luther's Seelsorge. Theologie in der Vielfalt der Lebenssituationen an seinen Briefen dargestellt* (Tübingen: J. C. B. Mohr [Paul Siebeck], 1997).

Never more penetratingly has this theme been represented than by Oscar Wilde in *The Picture of Dorian Gray* (1884). Dorian Gray, the seemingly eternal youthful hero, lives a life of high aesthetic feeling linked with a self-justifying and contemptuous destruction of other people's lives. A portrait of Gray, locked away high in an attic room, magically bears the scars and warts of his disfigured and disfiguring life. The transfer is perfect, right through to the end.

> The picture itself — that was evidence. He would destroy it. . . . Once it had given him pleasure to watch it changing and growing old. Of late he had felt no such pleasure. It had kept him awake at night. When he had been away, he had been filled with terror lest other eyes should look upon it. . . . It had been like conscience to him. Yes, it had been conscience. He would destroy it.
>
> He looked round, and saw the knife. . . . It would kill the past, and when that was dead he would be free. It would kill this monstrous soul-life, and, without its hideous warnings, he could be at peace. He seized the thing, and stabbed the picture with it.
>
> There was a cry heard, and a crash. The cry was so horrible in its agony that the frightened servants woke, and crept out of their rooms. . . .
>
> When they entered they found, hanging upon the wall, a splendid portrait of their master as they had last seen him, in all the wonder of his exquisite youth and being. Lying on the floor was a dead man, in evening dress, with a knife in his heart. He was withered, wrinkled, and loathsome of visage. It was not till they had examined the rings that they recognized who it was.

The one who is "sold under sin" (Romans 7:14) is the one who must pay the price of death. The human predicament is that disastrous.

Continuing History

Having noted the theme of a blood-guilt transfer in literature, in the "textbook" case of *The Picture of Dorian Gray*, we can observe it making its way, like the worm that turns, through the history of thought, in particular through the history of Christian thought. Consider the tradition of thought concerning the universal immobility of human nature under capital sentence, which is connected with St. Augustine of Hippo (354-430). This tradition of thought flourished within Roman Catholicism until the Jesuit order succeeded in manipulating political circumstances to persuade the pope to disallow the Augustinian teaching. The Jesuits' chief adversaries at that time (the late seventeenth and early eighteenth centuries) were called the Jansenists. The Jansenists portrayed with conviction and insight the true colors, as they saw them, of the human bondage to capital judgment. Thus Philippe Nicole's tormented picture of the general human misfortune:

> The world as a whole is a place of torture. Let us imagine a great big room, full of every conceivable instrument of human torture. It is a huge place, but dark and hard to see in. But there is one man I see whose whole purpose in life consists of filling and re-filling that room with vipers and snakes.[5]

The Augustinian current died out in Roman Catholicism after 1713, which is the year of the Jesuit triumph embodied in the papal "constitution" or ruling *Unigenitus*. The Augustinian tradition, while dead in the Roman Church, continued within the Reformation churches in various forms. The conviction continues to be that the depth, magnitude, and widespread character of sin calls upon itself the sentence of death from God, not because he wishes it but because he must be just in order to be God. Experience, literature, and theology — and most specifically the Bible — understand the human being as incapable of improvement, thus caught in the bondage of sin, open to the fatal consequence, the bands of death, to quote the Luther hymn ("Christ lay in the bands of death") and the J. S. Bach cantata deriving from it. The result is that human existence is a cul-de-sac from which the only exit is either suicide or guilt-transfer. The subjective and also the objective culpability of human experience

5. P. Nicole, "Essais de Morale" (1671), as cited in T. de Sainte-Beuve, *Port Royal*, vol. 2 (Paris: Gallimard, 1953), p. 224; my translation.

renders life without Christ a Damocles-sword mode of existence, for which the best description would have to be acute and chronic anxiety.

Christ, therefore, had to die for our sins. The thesis holds: Christ *died* for our sins.

Thesis 17: *Christ* died for our sins.

The human situation — our original sin and the sins that grow from it — is catastrophic, tragic, and extreme. It requires an extreme solution: Christ's death, the guilt-transfer of blood in death and life.

The Incarnation

Classically speaking, we have gone from the teaching concerning original sin to the teaching concerning penal substitutionary atonement. We proceed now to a discussion of who it is that died. We proceed now from the atonement to the incarnation. We are proceeding from the impact upon the human race, the human beings, of what has been done — the existential aspect, one could say — to the person, rather the Person, who has done this magnificent thing. The method here could be understood as a theology from the ground up, although that would not be completely accurate, since we have begun with the interplay between empirically verifiable fact (original sin) and what the Bible teaches about human bondage (also original sin). Properly speaking, *the ground floor of this theology is atonement.* From atonement we must ask the same question the scribes asked after Jesus healed the paralytic in Mark's Gospel: "Who can forgive sins but God alone?" (2:7).

Right theology — that is, theology that is not abstraction — proceeds from action to ontology, and not the other way around. Jesus died, his death was effective, he met our overwhelming and so highly threatening need. Therefore, who could he be but God? It comes down to that. Jesus' being confirms the saving event he achieved. Ontology corroborates

69

soteriology. His divinity ratifies his death. Only if he were divine could the death be an effective work. To be sure, the incarnation preceded the atonement in the "mind," if we may call it that, of God. "He came down to earth from heaven" (Cecil Frances Alexander, "Once in Royal David's City"). The birth preceded the death. But from our point of view, from the side of our experience of God, from the ground up, the death precedes the birth. The birth is only of interest when linked to its effect.

Similarly, the death derives its virtue from the perfection of the One who died. It was necessary for him to be perfect — that is, the God who also is perfect — in order for the atonement to take place. Thus Cecil Frances Alexander proves helpful again: "There was no other good enough/To pay the price of sin,/He only could unlock the gate/of heav'n, and let us in" ("There Is a Green Hill Far Away").

What, then, can we say concerning the being of the Christ, the being of the Christ who died? Whoever he is, he is predicated in this theology by one most important fact: he died a substitutionary sacrifice for the original sin and the actual sins of the world. In order for the sacrifice to take hold, the object sacrificed must be perfect. Because God alone is perfect (i.e., "Who but God can forgive sins?" — Mark 2:7; Luke 5:21), the claim that the sacrifice of the substitutionary atonement has been accepted implies without condition that God was in Christ (2 Corinthians 5:19). Thus we have the emergence in theological reflection of the incarnation. Incarnation, in theological reflection, is the afterbirth of the atonement. The incarnation is the consequence of the atonement, its logical corollary.

This does not contradict the "salvation-history" progression, even the purely temporal progression, of incarnation to atonement, for the historical birth obviously precedes the historical death. Nevertheless, in right theology, theology rightfully conducted from "the ground up," atonement precedes incarnation. Thus the incarnation is subordinate to the atonement. More precisely stated, the incarnation is subordinate, both in theological time and in existential impact, to the atonement.[6]

---

6. The nineteenth-century Anglican theologian E. A. Litton (1813-1897) wrote these strong words about the proper ordering of atonement and incarnation: "Romanism (in-

We ought to concede, further, that the incarnation is abstract to a degree that the atonement is not. Soteriology is more concrete than ontology. Nevertheless, God became man!

The Trinity

A further development from **Thesis 17,** that *Christ* died for our sins, is the doctrine of the Trinity. Here we proceed to an even higher level of abstraction. The doctrine of the Trinity is a reflection on the doctrine of the incarnation, which in its turn is a reflection on the successful substitutionary atonement of Christ on the cross. The Trinity is a complicated and notoriously abstruse and enigmatic concept by which the single Being of God is understood to exist in community. The Trinity, which can be elucidated only with imagination from the New Testament as there are only two texts that refer to it (2 Corinthians 13:14 and Matthew 28:19), builds on the two-nature theory of Jesus Christ. This is the theory that he had both a human nature and a divine nature. If God and Jesus were two natures of a single unified Being, then that also implies a separation between God and Jesus in the same Person. The historic explanation of this separation, the historic explanation of its possibility, is that God the Father and Jesus the Son of God are two Persons within one unified God. The Holy Spirit, referred to often in the Bible, both in the Old and New Testaments, becomes from our human point of view the presence of both the other two Persons of God in history *since the Ascension.* This we have already stated. If the Holy Spirit is the true expression

---

cluding its mutilated counterpart, Anglo-Catholicism) is a religion of the incarnation, the virtue of which is communicated by sacraments; Protestantism is a religion of the atonement, the virtue of which is appropriated by direct faith in Christ, His Word and His works. . . . On neither side are these cordial facts of religion, or their connexion, denied; there could have been no atonement, if there had not been an incarnation; but the stress laid on the one or the other, . . . may affect one's whole conception of Christianity and lead to widely divergent theological systems" (xiv). See Litton's *Introduction to Dogmatic Theology,* which presents in classic systematized form the subordination of incarnation to atonement (London: James Clarke & Co., 1960).

both of God the Father and of God the Son in their absence from the human theater, then God the Spirit must be of equal substance with the Son and the Father. The result of this progression of thinking is this: there are three Persons in one God.

The Trinity is a reflection on the incarnation as the incarnation is a reflection on the atonement. The negative reactions to Trinitarianism within the Christian tradition are easy to understand. Such reactions to Trinitarianism have also come from within Islam, which has as its historic point of origin a sort of counter-reformation to Christian Trinitarianism misunderstood as tritheism. Negative reactions to Trinitarianism both within and outside the church are easy to understand. They are easy to understand not just because of the illogicality of the three-in-one conception, but also because of its metaphysical abstraction, which seems to exist at a level detached from direct human experience.

Trinitarian thinking does fall into place, however, in the light of the absence in the world of the risen Christ's presence. That is, the Trinity makes sense if we posit or understand the Holy Spirit as the perceived stand-in for the God of faith, the vicar of faith in the wake of Jesus' ascension to heaven. There is an irresistible three-ness to the action of God if you draw a theological timeline up to the birth (God the Father), from the birth through the death-resurrection-ascension (God the Son), through Pentecost and right through to the final and heavenly kingdom of God (God the Holy Spirit). The end of the Holy Spirit, from our human point of view, comes on the other side of our human death.

Even so, despite timelines of salvation history and all varieties of explanation offered by the ancient fathers of the church, the Trinity of all core Christian doctrines requires the highest degree of abstraction. Is it essential to Christian theology?

The church historian Adolph von Harnack (1851-1930) made an important statement in the fourth edition of his famous book *What Is Christianity?* (1899/1900):

If redemption is to be traced to Christ's person and work, everything would seem to depend upon a right understanding of this person together with what he accomplished. The formation of a correct theory of and about Christ threatens to assume the position of chief importance, and to pervert the majesty and simplicity of the Gospel. . . . No long period elapsed before it was taught in the Church that the all-important thing is to know how the person of Jesus was constituted, what sort of physical nature he had, and so on. . . . This did not affect Paul's right to epitomize the gospel in the message of Christ crucified, thus exhibiting God's power and wisdom. . . . There are thousands today in whom the Christian faith is still propagated in the same manner, namely, through Christ. But to demand assent to a series of propositions about Christ's person is a different thing altogether.[7]

Harnack's worry concerning the New Testament rooting of the doctrine of the incarnation is doubly, triply valid concerning the New Testament footings for the doctrine of the Trinity. It is an unhappy fact that Christianity became absorbed for more than three centuries in the question of God's Trinity. The Trinity is an important theory insofar as it safeguards Christ's divinity, which in turn confirms the atonement. But it is too intellectual in its essence to fuel the Christian movement. It is too speculative to motivate mission and too distant to provide immediate hope and comfort to the hopeless and the comfortless.

Thesis 18: The Trinity is the last development in the logic of systematic theology.

The Hardest Part

A further important matter remains from the picture of God that is built up from the portrait of Christ we have been considering in the sentence "Christ died for our sins." This is the question of God's prior intention or "motive," so to speak, in his sending of Christ. In order for God to be the

---

7. As quoted in *Adolph von Harnack: Liberal Theology at Its Height,* ed. Martin Rumscheidt (London: Collins, 1989), p. 179.

motive force behind the blood of Christ and the atonement, the root cause and prior existence of Christ before the incarnation, and speculatively described as "Triune," God must be a *flexible* entity. God in his relationship to the human being and to the history of human beings must be understood as dynamic, in relationship, in conversation or two-way give-and-take, and therefore as open-ended. For God to have birthed the incarnation strategy, for God to have created the atonement strategy, for God to be predicated as Three-in-One, God must be a Being capable of movement and transition.

God as predicated by the shedding of the blood of Christ must have affect. God must have feeling. God must have sorrow. God must be capable of having compassion that responds to human distress (i.e., Exodus 3:7). He must be capable even of dividedness — or better, a variety of emotions. He responds to our bondage by means of the death and life of Christ. "God is love" (1 John 4:8). The whole characterization of God allowed us by virtue of the New Testament's portrait of Jesus requires us to say, in the formal language of theology, that God is *passible.* "When Jesus saw Mary weeping, and the Jews who came with her also weeping, he was deeply moved in spirit and troubled even; . . . Jesus wept. . . . Then Jesus, deeply moved again, came to the tomb" (John 11:33, 35, 38). We need go no further than the Jesus of the Gospels to see the atonement of divine compassion.

This means that God in Christian theology does not have feet of concrete.[8] He is not stuck in or held captive to the metaphysical category of changelessness. While we cannot discover in the Bible the idea that God is in development or process, that is, not yet fully realized but *becoming,* we do in Scripture run up unmistakably against the understanding of God as being in relationship with humanity. God is in relationship to humanity principally in the sending of Christ to die for the many. He is also in relationship to humanity in the engagement of prayer.

---

8. Jürgen Moltmann objected that the theologian Karl Rahner had set God in "feet of concrete" by virtue of his teaching on the impassibility of God. See Moltmann's *In der Geschichte der dreieinigen Gottes. Beiträge zur trinitarischen Theologie* (Munich: Chr. Kaiser Verlag, 1991), pp. 171-72. For a summary of Moltmann's important teaching on the passibility of God, see the same book, pp. 45-53, and, most importantly, pp. 54-58.

The blood implies the incarnation implies the Trinity implies the God who suffers, who is moved, and who feels. The atonement as first principle of theology points to the Christian picture of the cosmic, suffering God. This picture of the suffering, crucified God is expressed well within Chaplain Geoffrey Studdert-Kennedy's poem from the First World War entitled "The Sorrow of God." The speaker in the poem is a "cockney" sergeant at the Front, looking over at a "little boy corporal" lying dead in the mud:

> Look at 'im lyin' there all uv a 'eap,
>> Wi' the blood soaken over 'is 'ead,
> Like a beautiful picture spoiled by a fool,
>> A bundle o' nothin' — dead.
> And it ain't only 'im — there's a mother at 'ome,
>> And 'e were the pride of 'er life.
> For it's women as pays in a thousand ways
>> For the madness o' this 'ere strife.
> And the lovin' God 'E looks down on it all,
>> On the blood and the mud and the smell.
> O God, if it's true, 'ow I pities you,
>> For ye must be livin' i' 'ell.
> You must be livin' i' 'ell all day,
>> And livin' i' 'ell all night.
> I'd rather be dead, wiv a 'ole through my 'ead,
>> I would, by a damn long sight,
> Than be livin' wi' you on your 'eavenly throne,
>> Lookin' down on yon bloody 'eap
> That were once a boy full o' life and joy,
>> And 'earin' 'is mother weep.
> *The sorrows o' God must be 'ard to bear*
>> *If 'E really 'as Love in 'Is 'eart,*
> *And the 'ardest part i' the world to play*
>> *Must surely be God's part.* (emphasis added)

Thesis 19: The atonement conveys the God who is moved both by the suffering and by the sin of the world.

The Atoned, Atoning God

> Down in the depth of mine iniquity,
> That ugly centre of infernal spirits;
> Where each sin feels her own deformity,
> In these particular torments she inherits,
>   Depriv'd of human graces, and divine,
>   Even there appears this saving God of mine.
>
> And in this fatal mirror of transgression,
> Shows men as fruit of his degeneration,
> The error's ugly infinite impression,
> Which bears the faithless down to desperation,
>   Depriv'd of human graces and divine,
>   Even there appears this saving God of mine.
>
> In power and truth, almighty and eternal,
> Which on the sin reflects strange desolation,
> With glory scourging all the sprites infernal,
> And unwanted hell with unprivation;
>   Depriv'd of human graces, not divine,
>   Even there appears this saving God of mine.
>
>   Fulke Greville[9]

The horrendous case of the human race under judgment requires the sacrifice of blood and substitution that occurred by means of the cross in time (**Theses 12-16**). The implication of such an absolutely necessary event is the presence of God in the Protagonist, Jesus Christ (**Thesis 17**).

---

9. Fulke Greville (1554-1628), *Selected Writings,* ed. Joan Rees (London: Athlone Press, 1973), pp. 43-44.

This leads to the doctrine of the incarnation. Only a divine being can effect atonement. Thus God is an atoning God. The dynamic or working spring of this substitution requires a Subject and an Object, the atoning God and the atoned God. God is "split" in two by his requirement of perfection in the human being. There are therefore two natures in Jesus and also two Persons in God. For the presence of God's absence within the intervening years, from the ascension to the present moment, there must be a third development in God, a third Person. This third Person is the Holy Spirit. The existence of the Spirit requires that we take a further step, the step of understanding God as Trinity (**Thesis 18**). This third step is speculative. But it is no more speculative than any other understanding of God that we might be given during the great interim, the period between A.D. 29 and our personal death, or, on a larger canvass, the period between A.D. 29 and the final coming of God to be all in all (1 Corinthians 15:24-28).

Within this scheme of the atoning, atoned God, we have also underlined his passibility, an open-endedness in God by which he hears and responds to the sufferings of people. He is touched by them and is by no means aloof (**Thesis 19**). "I have seen the affliction of my people who are in Egypt, and have heard their cry because of their taskmasters; I know their sufferings, and I have come down to deliver them" (Exodus 3:7-8).

It is now to the Christian life, the experienced outworking of the atonement-centered theology, that we proceed — to the dynamic of the atoned-for life, the "blood-bought" life (William Cowper). This life is theological existence in the true sense! It is the self-critical life and in classic terms the repentant life. It is the life lived before the mirror of what St. James calls the "law of liberty" (1:25). It is the meeting point of reality (our life as it is) and grace (our life as God has reconfigured it by means of his death). This meeting point, between life as it is and life as God imputes it to us through Christ, is what theology also calls Christian liberty, the *libertas christiana*. Liberty is not only the clearest way of describing the actual character of the Christian's existence before God, but it also describes the method of theology. The paradigm of Christian living will prove to be the paradigm for all theological thinking.

CHAPTER THREE

The Method of Theology
and the Method of Life:
Libertas christiana

The position of the theologian, . . . is exactly the same as that of
any other Christian in his particular calling. . . . One becomes a
theologian in the true sense by dint of that capacity which is
called in Paul "the distinguishing of true spirits from false." . . .
This is nothing over and above what is laid upon the whole
Christian community and upon each one of its members.[1]

Ernst Käsemann

Criticism involves inquiry into the essence of Christianity together with
inquiring into the period of time in which it first emerged. Criticism is
the means by which this task is to be achieved. Criticism also has its stim-
ulus in the gospel message. It serves the cause of theological truth and
seeks to build up the Christian community.

The requirements for criticism are threefold: first, that it be bound
by no dogmatic assumption that might disturb the impartiality of its
judgment; second, that it validate nothing as historical truth that cannot

1. "Theologians and Laity," in *New Testament Questions of Today* (London: SCM Press,
1969), pp. 294-95.

be demonstrated from the extant sources; and finally, that it never lose sight of the universal.[2]

Luther inaugurated critical theology. He opened the way to the *freedom of theology*. Luther accomplished this by applying to the inherited Scriptures, in the spirit of acute self-criticism before God, a standard that he understood to be the gospel. He interpreted the whole of Scripture by means of one interpretive principle: the gospel of God's justification of the human being or sinner.[3] This gospel of justification became the material principle of change in the church. It became the lens through which the Scriptures were to be understood, both as a whole and also in part. The gospel interpreted the Scriptures, which in turn became the formal instrument for evaluating and criticizing the church. The gospel also became the standard for canonicity, by which certain sections of Scripture could be understood to be less pertinent, less pastoral, less inspired than others.

It is no good complaining that Luther established a "canon within the canon" in respect to this overwhelming emphasis on a single material principle. Every theologian works from a canon within the canon. Every preacher, every reader of Scripture, in fact, works from a canon within the canon. One of the purposes of this short systematic theology is to declare the common ground between theologians and ordinary readers in the Christian life and movement. What applies in general to the common reader applies specifically to the theological thinker. He or she begins with Jesus of Nazareth, moves to the great question of the presence in his absence of the risen Christ, is arrested by the single interpretative and unifying principle of the blood atonement, and arrives finally at the place of meeting with God in the emotions and in the mind, which is always the place of self-criticism. Self-criticism before God is another way of saying repentance and faith.

2. See Roy A. Harrisville and Walter Sundberg, *The Bible in Modern Culture* (Grand Rapids: Eerdmans, 1995), p. 113.

3. Luther's understanding of the proper subordination of the words of God to the Word of God as forgiveness and justification can be seen comprehensively yet within a short space by consulting his prefaces to the books of the Bible, which he composed between 1522 and 1541. See his *Vorreden zur Bibel*, ed. by Heinrich Bornkamm (Göttingen: Vandenhoeck & Ruprecht, 1989).

Self-criticism without the mirror of Christian liberty, that is, without forgiveness (James 1:23-25), would be both fruitless and despairing. On the other hand, forgiveness, the reflection of humanity's plight from the point of view of the face of God in Christ, the countenance that reflects back a different picture than the one received by the mirror, would be superficial and unpenetrating without the self-criticism that must precede it. Therefore, the place of meeting or the "holy of holies" is always the same for everyone: *self-criticism before God in the light of freedom from judgment.* These two things occur in the gospel at the same time, in urgent simultaneous relation. This is true for theologians in the same degree as it is true for anyone else in the Christian religion. It is another way of saying that the canon of interpretation for theological work is the canon of critical self-analysis. This is the principle behind all proper reflection on our human experience. The result is freedom.

This is the true enlightenment that the North European Enlightenment of the eighteenth century believed it was in the way of achieving. We are not postmodernists, therefore, in regard to freedom. We wish to uplift the gospel of freedom, this *libertas,* in every sphere of life, in its New Testament exclamation (Galatians 5:1). This principle of freedom is able to create a unity to all intellectual work that is critical, self-critical, God-critical, text-critical, and is yet the truth that sets us free (John 8:32).

Thesis 20: The theological method is the same as the method that has been given to "test the spirits" (1 John 4:1) in the life of every Christian. This method is the gospel, which starts with self-criticism (i.e., repentance) and turns the human being by means of grace to the works of love. The gospel of the forgiveness of sin is the first principle of all theological thinking.

Christians are much more than guilty people awaiting pardon for their transgressions of the divine law. They are beings inwardly confronting themselves and aiming to go beyond all worldly misfortune, their own faults being the most sensitive focal point of this misfortune. It is through this tormenting responsibility that Christians are in their inwardness individuals, and not simply subjugated beings destined to be punished or rewarded by an unrelenting god.[4]

Thesis 21: The method of theology grounded in self-criticism and in the confidence of forgiveness from God produces freedom. This freedom fosters the inductive study of all ideas and all phenomena.

The starting point for the method of theology is also its end point. It is the freedom to investigate and confront the phenomena of life from the standpoint of a freedom given prior to that extensive freedom, the prior freedom being the forgiveness of sins by virtue of the blood of Christ. This first freedom disables the agendas of the subjective human being, by which he or she is chronically seeking to bring reality into harmony with already-held *idées fixes*.

Idées fixes are intrinsically neurotic concepts because they are deductive. They are prior conceptions frequently derived from inward, often unspoken needs. Because of their subjectivity, *idées fixes* require dismantling. The only enduring means by which they can be dismantled permanently is through an end to the fear that generates them. This is almost always some form of the fear of judgment. That fear has been seized by the atonement of Christ and thrown off. In the new being created by the blood, or rather in the new being enabled by the blood, the liberty of what the world terms "openness" is engendered.

The Epistle of St. James offers a memorable picture of the relation between the liberty of forgiveness and the freedom of action that flows from it.

Be doers of the word, and not hearers only, deceiving yourselves. For if any one is a hearer of the word and not a doer, he is like a man who ob-

---

4. Marcel Gauchet, *The Disenchantment of the World: A Political History of Religion* (Princeton: Princeton University Press [New French Thought], 1997), p. 167.

serves his natural face in a mirror; for he observes himself and goes away and at once forgets what he was like. But he who looks into the perfect law, the law of liberty, and perseveres, being no hearer that forgets but a doer that acts, he shall be blessed in his doing. (1:22-25)

The basis for integration and fruitfulness is the termination of self-deception. This is accomplished only when the truth is viewed by the self-deceiver in the light of liberty, the liberty of the children of God. St. James is saying in his way exactly what St. John says concerning the connection between truth-telling in the light of grace and the love that is the direct result of truth-telling:

If we say we have no sin, we deceive ourselves, and the truth is not in us. If we confess our sins, he is faithful and just, and will forgive our sins and cleanse us from all unrighteousness. . . . By this we may be sure that we are in him: he who says he abides in him ought to walk in the same way in which he walked. (1 John 1:8-9; 2:5-6)

The connection between theological method and the *libertas christiana* that is the birthright of all Christians should now be clear. The connection is from blood to freedom, from forgiveness to a love that exists not from constraint but rather from desire. The poet William Cowper, whose hymn "There is a Fountain" has already conveyed in quintessence the atonement core of theology, expresses also in quintessence the movement from blood to love within the context of freedom.

How long beneath the Law I lay
    In bondage and distress;
I toiled the precept to obey,
    But toiled without success.
Then all my servile works, were done
    A righteousness to raise;
Now, freely chosen in the Son,
    I freely choose His way.

To see the law by Christ fulfilled,
   And hear His pardoning voice,
Changes a slave into a child,
   And duty into choice.

                   "Love Constraining to Obedience," 1777

The analogy of theological method to "regular" daily Christian existence is a central principle of this short systematic theology. It is the reason why this book can be a short one. If the fruit of the blood's watering the earth is liberty, then all explaining, interpreting, and creative thinking stem from that. It is not up to any one theology or theologian to spell out the consequences. They vary in numberless ways and extend with very long spokes from one organizing hub. The organizing hub is liberty derived from blood.

Interestingly, Luther never wrote a systematic theology. Yet almost everything in theology can be derived from his massive exegetical and occasional works. Once he had come upon the exact organizing and unifying principle, the rest flowed as time and the requirements of occasion dictated. For Luther the unifying principle was God's justification of sinners through Christ's atonement, with the resulting freedom of the Christian. With that principle always in view, the Reformer never needed to organize the rest of his thought. This is the essential model for all theology that is free.

Thesis 22: The inductive method is the method of Christian theology. Therefore, theology is not a received truth.

The freedom of theology is not inaugurated for purposes of the vindication or verification of answers the theologian already possesses. This is why theology required the Reformation. Luther ended the reign of dogmatic theology because his understanding of justification drew back the curtain separating the possibility of atonement from its realization. Freedom from judgment, and therefore from all preexisting judgments, was achieved by the atonement of Christ on the cross.

In the light of that mission which is "the law of liberty" (James 1:25), it was no longer necessary to adhere to preconditions, that is, to dogma. Adolph von Harnack believed that the Reformer's understanding of the gospel brought to a close the history of Christian dogma. The mediating necessity of dogma was obviated in the light of personal and corporate justification by faith. *Henceforth, theology would operate in principle as an open system.* It could encounter the text of the Bible in its complexity without fear of losing its faith in God. It could encounter the phenomena of the external world without fear of contradiction. That the scientific revolution occurred in conjunction with the Reformation's cry of freedom should not surprise. That the beginnings of republicanism coincide with the dispersion of Reformation insights should not surprise. The tale is told on the reliefs of the once-famous Reformation monument at Geneva. There is a clean line from the Ninety-Five Theses of 1517 at Wittenberg to the Glorious Revolution of 1688 in England.

In the Protestant Episcopal Church in the United States, a small segment of the world's Christian community, this particular insight concerning Christian liberty and the method of theology became a driving one through the ministry of the celebrated late-nineteenth-century preacher Phillips Brooks (1835-1893). His watchword, which remains sculpted in marble over the altar of Trinity Church, Copley Square, Boston, was the words of Jesus from John 8:32: "Ye shall know the truth, and the truth will make you free." Brooks had derived his *libertas christiana* in theology from his teacher at the Virginia Seminary, William Sparrow. Sparrow's headstone bears *his* great text: "Seek the truth, come whence it may, cost what it will." The importance of the example of Sparrow and Brooks is the fruitful nature of their starting point, freedom. That struck a chord with thousands and thousands of people and became a cornerstone of "Broad-Church" or "liberal" theology in America.

The negative within that vastly influential example in the American reception of the *libertas christiana* was its disconnection from the blood atonement. Because the Christian freedom of late-nineteenth-century theology ran parallel with its rejection of the older "evangelical" teaching concerning the substitutionary atonement, the foundation of this freedom was weaker than the foundation of Luther and most of the other Reformers. Without the blood atonement, Christian liberty became doctrinaire. It therefore turned into law, even self-righteousness, within a generation. When the *libertas* of self-criticism tied to the inductive method loses its connection with its instrumental cause, the substitutionary atonement, it becomes vulnerable to the position of seeing the speck in the other person's eye as opposed to the log in one's own.

This short systematic theology seeks to ground the liberty of thought in the forgiveness of sins.

Thesis 23: In theology without constraints, tradition, on the one hand, and church, on the other, always play secondary roles.

Free inductive theology demythologizes tradition and demythologizes church. Tradition is always secondary to the gospel of blood atonement and to the freedom of reason created from it. Human traditions are a crazy weave of outdated circumstances, past idiosyncrasies, unexamined ideas that have somehow over time accumulated the weight of authority, and passed-down "wisdoms." These are all another name for law. They bind individuals, and they bind theology. This is what Jesus said about tradition as such:

> Why do you [scribes and Pharisees] transgress the commandment of God for the sake of your tradition? . . . For the sake of your tradition, you have made void the word of God. (Matthew 15:3, 6; see also Mark 7:8-9, 13)

The epistles of St. Paul repeat the criticism:

> For you have heard of my former life in Judaism, how I persecuted the church of God violently and tried to destroy it; and I advanced in Judaism beyond many of my own age among my people, so extremely zealous was I for the traditions of my fathers. (Galatians 1:13-14)

See to it that no one makes a prey of you by philosophy and empty deceit, according to human traditions. (Colossians 2:8)

Jesus criticizes the traditions of the Jews to the extent that they run counter to the overwhelming evidence of the mind of God as set out in the Scriptures as a whole. Paul is also critical of the traditions of his inherited faith. Paul, however, also sees the looming power of tradition when it comes from a very different quarter: Greek or Hellenistic *idées fixes* concerning cosmology and philosophy.

The liberty of criticism accords with the freedom inherent in the forgiven life. This liberty has no realms from which it is excluded by taboo or commonly accepted exception. This is the demythologizing trend in Christianity. It is the meaning behind the famous story of the boy who spoke the truth that everyone else was thinking but was afraid to say: "Father, why is the emperor wearing no clothes?" The others were silent not because of ignorance or blindness, but because of subjugation and fear. The Christian has nothing to fear. Love may stop his or her mouth, as in Paul's tender words to the Corinthian Christians to the effect that they are to concede their "rights" to eat meat that has been sacrificed to idols out of respect for the weaker, less liberated brother or sister (1 Corinthians 8). Love may sometimes retard the demythologizing process and soften its impact. But in principle, the Christian will always question human precepts.

The church, too, stands under the judgment of blood-bought inductive freedom. A survey of the church's history reveals that it, like other institutions, has frequently departed from its founding principle — the first commandment to have no other god but the Lord, whose chief intention to grace is declared in the atonement of Christ. The church has departed so far from its first principles, in fact, on so many occasions and through so many periods, that one can fairly observe that it has seldom been the church in anything like its true or ideal form. Thus Klaus Scholder's observation on church orthodoxy as embodied over the long view of Christian history still stands:

> [It is the] experience of church history, that in times of supreme changes the church is not saved by the erection of external defenses but only by

going back to its theological center. Thus in the fourth century only a few communities may really have been able to follow the strict formulae of Nicaea; and in fact only a few supporters of the Reformation will have adopted Luther's doctrine of grace in all its radical nature.[5]

The demythologizing liberty to criticize that flows from the doctrine of God's grace has too seldom been administered. The Barmen Confession in 1934 is a recent outstanding example, as is the Alabama Christian Movement for Human Rights from 1956 to 1964.

Reasoned freedom of inquiry demythologizes all penultimates. It also de-objectifies the church. Church *in principle* is in its ideal expression the coming together of two realities: the cross of Christ and Christian freedom. These two ideas jointly create families of love over and over and over again through time. To overestimate church as a value in itself is to objectify the non-objectifiable and thus to possess that which can never be possessed. "Far from depicting the original healer of pure nature free of all contradiction, the church is caught in the fragile and sinful; it is not an external idea, but a temporal means."[6]

Thesis 24: The critical method, both in theology and in daily life, exorcizes the world of false gods and false assumptions.

Church in its ideality touches down in history, like a Texas tornado, with the appearance of caprice, making contact with time and space, yet then withdrawing almost as quickly as it came. Thus we confront the painful facts of totally empty Christian churches turned into mosques and museums in North Africa. Thus we have to confront the hundreds upon hundreds of Nonconformist chapels in Wales that are now defunct or turned

5. Klaus Scholder, *The Churches and the Third Reich*, vol. 2 (Philadelphia: Fortress Press, 1988), p. 155.

6. F. W. J. Schelling, in his discussion of Schleiermacher's *Christmas Eve*, vol. 7 (Stuttgart: J. G. Cotta, 1860), p. 508; as cited in Harrisville and Sundberg, *The Bible in Modern Culture*, p. 83.

to use as private residences. Thus we have to confront the dozens of Reformed churches in the Netherlands that are now well-trafficked health clubs. Thus too Lebanon, which only a few decades ago was the thriving center of Maronite Christianity; thus the Palestinian Christian churches, struggling to survive in what was once their own province; thus the huge arks of "mainline" churches in emptied-out American city centers; thus the ancient Saxon brick churches of Romania. The list is inexhaustibly defeating.

Yet we also have to confront the "fact on the ground" of the crowded, open-straw churches of East Africa, packed and jammed with their Christian multitudes, and the overflowing house churches of China, caught up in a revival beyond numbering. We have to confront the thousands of store-front evangelical and Pentecostal church communities in South and Central America, and the gleaming new independent churches of suburban America, warehouse-style buildings with "cathedral" facades. The tornado of God's fervent rush comes and goes through world history. Any geography of Christian church growth will immediately demythologize any traditions we still possess of a standing army of Christian believers and institutions. History's criticism is free and unthreatened. This is due to the cessation of judgment by virtue of Christ's cross. Demythologizing, understood as the unconstrained right of criticism based on freedom from *idées fixes,* is the handmaid of Christianity's forward movement.

Final Thesis (25): The world exists in the time between the blood of Christ and our death. The Spirit acts in the present through freedom enacted within the works of love.

Conclusion

The wholesale reconstruction of human space under the influence of God's paradoxical absolutization/withdrawal is the hidden source behind the expanding fragmented components of our democratic, individualizing, state-based, historical, technological, capitalist world.

Marcel Gauchet

Luther did not hand over something complete and finished to Christendom, but set before it a problem, to be developed out of many encumbering surroundings, to be continuously dealt with in connection with the entire life of the Spirit and with the social condition of mankind, but to be solved only in faith itself.

Adolph von Harnack

This short systematic theology roots all theological inquiry in the historical Jesus. It is a risky foundation when the records of his life are constantly being questioned and pared down. But it is a venture of faith. This theology rests everything on a basic picture of Jesus that accords completely in spirit with the celebrated nineteenth-century sculpture by Bertel Thorvaldsen entitled "The Compassionate Christ" (1821). We have to be willing to venture everything on the validity of the portrait of the "friend of sinners" found in the Gospels. "God's grace is only manifest in the historical work of the historical Christ."[1]

The problem of Christ's ascension, or disappearance from the human point of view, becomes *the* great problem for theology at its starting point. We affirmed the presence of Christ's absence in the interim between the ascension and our own disappearance (i.e., by reason of our personal death or the return of Christ to mediate the kingdom of God in history once and for all). We located this peculiar presence in the works of love performed by forgiven sinners. This affirmation ran parallel with the Reformers' understanding that works are the fruits of divine love in the world that spring naturally and unself-consciously from prior belovedness.

We located the Holy Spirit in the works of love. We also understood the Subject of theology to be God in Christ, the object of theology to be the human being, and the inferior subject of theology to be the devil.

From the Subject of theology to the content of theology, we passed from the divine Speaker to the Word spoken. The content of theology is the "Old, Old Story, of Jesus and His Love." The content of theology, sharpened to its great matter, is the substitutionary atonement of Christ on the cross. This is the hub from which all the spokes derive. All theories of systematic theology are developments from this heart of the matter.

Forgiveness is the result of the blood atonement of Christ. Forgiveness frees the heart and the mind from the fear of judgment, hence from the need to sustain *idées fixes.* Thus the theology of forgiveness creates the freedom of theology. The forgiven theologian is free to be inductive, and in principle *completely* inductive, rather than deductive. Forgiveness is the only first principle in the enterprise of theology. Theology is therefore open-ended — or, better, open to the phenomena of all that is other to the theologian. Not deductive, but rather inductive in its essence and in all its conclusions, theology is no different in quality from common Christian living. It is grounded in self-criticism, or repentance, from the

---

1. Adolph von Harnack, *History of Dogma,* vol. 7, trans. from the German edition by Neil Buchanan (New York: Dover, 1961), p. 198.

human point of view. It is grounded in acceptance or grace, from Christ's point of view. There are no taboos and no exceptions in the list of subjects and the forms of data that theology is able to engage. One corollary of this is that theology is in constant development as to its *object*, humanity and the world, but in constant reaffirmation as to its *Subject*, the crucified Christ of the Bible.

The conclusion of this short systematic theology, which has been the setting forth of twenty-five theses to root the work of Christian theologians, is nevertheless a question. It is a question that springs from Augustine's development as well as from Luther's, and indeed from St. Paul's. The question is this: What is the relationship between this theology of God's absence as his presence, which is radical because of its taking down of all mediatorial instruments, and the inherited Christian tradition, which both contains the kernel of such a theology and hardens a material of objectivity around that kernel? In other words, what is the relation between the radical core of Christianity and the conserving forms of its transmission?

The more radical Augustine became regarding the spiritual realities he conceived within the doctrines of God's grace in Christ and the bound will of the human being, the more conservative he became in issues of church order and authority. Luther, too, was the great innovator in the field of spiritual religion. Yet the longer he worked as a theologian, the more conservative he became in his impulses for dealing with issues of the day, especially when they boiled forth within his own Protestant camp. The same can be said of Pascal and the Jansenists in the seventeenth century. There is this consistent alliance, in the history of thought at least, between the affirmation of grace and the negation of change. Thus Augustine, Luther, and Pascal would all be quick to deny that the consequence of their insights concerning God should lead to "our democratic, individualizing, state-based, historical, technologized, capitalist world" (Gauchet).

But it has. And it does. The end of the mediatorial principle in religion, an end that is implicit in the "time that is coming when the true worshipers shall worship God in spirit and in truth" (John 4:23), leads to freedom in every field of human experience. This freedom is connected to the works of love, yet it is truly inductive. It creates discoverers and initiators in life rather than actors in a theater directed by the actions of another. Therefore the principle of non-mediated religion takes us into developments involving human assertion and even assertiveness. The Christian thinker often reels from the freedom that flows from the Christian insight concerning Christ. Thus a duality is present in theology that results in constant confrontation between the ancient Story and its Promethean implications. "Theology necessarily entails temptation, contestation and controversy."[2]

I offer no solution to this problem. It is the startling union of a radical experience of God that is described in its original form in ancient transmitted texts; of a spiritual, unseen religion linked to unpredictable results; of the bondage of human will freed for the purposes of human loving that will vary from context to context; of submission to the act of God that results in the breaking of chains all along the line of human experience. The only factor that is able to make this perpetual tension tolerable is the assurance of Christ, who promised to be present with us "always until the end of the age" (Matthew 28:20) and who has been hailed as forever contemporary in the words "Jesus Christ is the same, yesterday, today, and forever" (Hebrews 13:8). The compassionate Christ is the only One who ties all epochs and all the exercises of human freedom together into one consistent labor of love.

2. Oswald Bayer, "Worship and Theology," in *Worship and Ethics: Lutherans and Anglicans in Dialogue,* ed. Oswald Bayer and Alan Suggate (Berlin and New York: Walter de Gruyter, 1996), p. 160.

APPENDIX A

Beza's *Summa totius Christianismi*

Summa totius Christianismi, sive descriptio et distributio
causarum salutis electorum, et exitii reproborum, ex sacris literis collecta.

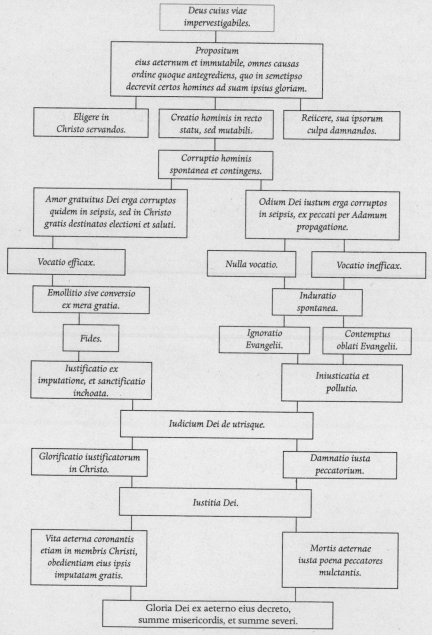

Beza's Summa totius Christianismi

A Summary of the Entire Christian Faith*

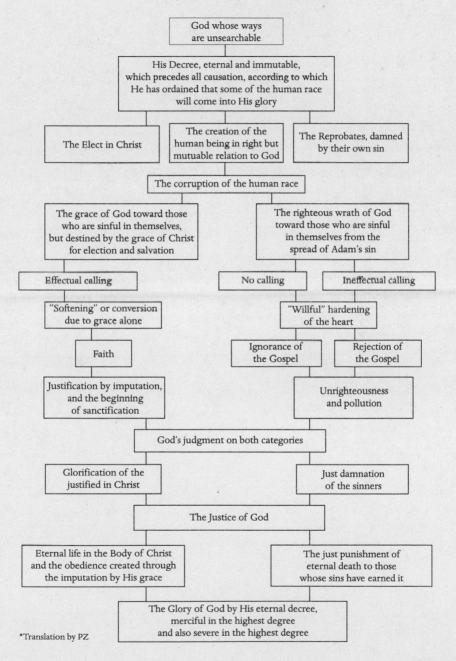

God whose ways are unsearchable

His Decree, eternal and immutable, which precedes all causation, according to which He has ordained that some of the human race will come into His glory

The Elect in Christ

The creation of the human being in right but mutuable relation to God

The Reprobates, damned by their own sin

The corruption of the human race

The grace of God toward those who are sinful in themselves, but destined by the grace of Christ for election and salvation

The righteous wrath of God toward those who are sinful in themselves from the spread of Adam's sin

Effectual calling

No calling

Ineffectual calling

"Softening" or conversion due to grace alone

"Willful" hardening of the heart

Faith

Ignorance of the Gospel

Rejection of the Gospel

Justification by imputation, and the beginning of sanctification

Unrighteousness and pollution

God's judgment on both categories

Glorification of the justified in Christ

Just damnation of the sinners

The Justice of God

Eternal life in the Body of Christ and the obedience created through the imputation by His grace

The just punishment of eternal death to those whose sins have earned it

The Glory of God by His eternal decree, merciful in the highest degree and also severe in the highest degree

*Translation by PZ

97

APPENDIX B

Lucas Cranach's
"The Old and the New Testament"

Lucas Cranach's representation of the gospel message is extremely clear-cut in his work entitled "The Old and the New Testament." The gospel message of law and grace, or sin and salvation, is depicted in *objective* terms and therefore represented mythologically. Nevertheless, we know that the artist understood himself to be part of the story, as he included a portrait of himself in his last version of this theme, which was completed by his son in Weimar in 1553. Cranach's 1529 woodcut is a visual summary of this short, systematic theology.

God is the Subject of history, and humankind is the object. There-fore God as Judge is over everything in the left-hand side of the work (i.e., "the Old Testament"). Another, inferior subject of history is the Devil, who, together with death personified, prods the man (i.e., Adam) toward the destiny of hell. The law, in its conscience-stirring role represented by Aaron and Moses holding the tables of the law, conspires with the Devil and death to consign the man to torment, which is represented by fire.

The right-hand side of the woodcut represents the New Testament: grace or salvation. The Subject is again God, who exists for the forgiven and therefore liberated sinner and who is represented to the sinner as Christ on the cross. He is all that the man can see, although the prophets — represented in condensed form by John the Baptist — aid in directing the man's sight. The blood spurts from Christ's side in a great shower that covers the Adam-man. A dove flies through the stream of blood, representing the unseen God now seen, concretely and in every individual case, in the form of Christ on the cross. Christ on the cross is the crucified God. Thus the unseen God (the Father) and the presence of his absence (the Spirit) are expressed through *one* Person, Christ on the cross.

The resurrection of Christ, represented on the extreme right, secures the transaction. This is why Christ on the cross is depicted as grounded in or founded on the rock tomb that has now been broken open. The main thing, which is the blood, is established by means of the broken tomb.

If the Cranach woodcut puts into visual form the content of Chapters 1 and 2 of this systematic theology, it also suggests the method of Chapter 3. All human pretensions or beliefs of self-security are prodded out of the Adam by means of the threefold threat of law, death, and the Devil. God observes and yet controls this drama. The dynamic of self-criticism or repentance — that is, the criticism of all penultimates or attempts to stand solid without God — are contained within this picture of absolute desperation. Nothing is absolute, save the blood of Christ, founded on the broken tomb. Nothing stands, save in this dynamic. The method of knowledge and the method of individual life are the method of judgment. There are no absolutes save the blood and the resurrection of Christ.

Selected Reading List

Allison, C. FitzSimons. *The Rise of Moralism: The Proclamation of the Gospel from Hooker to Baxter.* London: SCM, 1966.

Bayer, Oswald. *Leibliches Wort. Reformation und Neuzeit im Konflikt.* Tübingen: J. C. B. Mohr (Paul Siebeck), 1992.

————. *Theologie.* HST volume 1. Gütersloh: Gütersloher Verlagshaus, 1994.

————. "Worship and Theology." In *Worship and Ethics: Lutherans and Anglicans in Dialogue.* Edited by Oswald Bayer and Alan Suggate. Berlin and New York: Walter de Gruyter, 1996.

Carey, George. *The Gate of Glory.* London, Sydney, Auckland, Toronto: Hodder and Stoughton, 1986.

Chorley, E. Clowes. *Men and Movements in the American Episcopal Church.* New York: Scribner's, 1948.

Cowper, William, and John Newton. *Olney Hymns in Three Books.* 1779 Facsimile of original copy. Second edition. Olney: The Cowper and Newton Museum, 1984.

Davie, Donald, editor. *The New Oxford Book of Christian Verse.* Oxford and New York: Oxford University Press, 1981.

Denney, James. *The Death of Christ.* London: Tyndale, 1951.

Ebeling, Gerhard. *Luther's Seelsorge. Theologie in der Vielfalt der Lebenssituationen an seinen Briefen dargestellt.* Tübingen: J. C. B. Mohr (Paul Siebeck), 1997.

————. *Lutherstudien.* Volumes 1-3. *Disputatio de Homine.* Tübingen: J. C. B. Mohr (Paul Siebeck), 1989.

The First and Second Prayer Books of King Edward VI. Everyman edition. London: J. M. Dent & Sons, 1910.

Gauchet, Marcel. *The Disenchantment of the World: A Political History of Religion.* Princeton: Princeton University Press (New French Thought), 1997.

Harnack, Adolph von. *History of Dogma.* Volumes 6 and 7. New York: Dover, 1961.

Harrisville, Roy A., and Walter Sundberg. *The Bible in Modern Culture: Historical and Historical-Critical Method from Spinoza to Käsemann.* Grand Rapids: Eerdmans, 1995.

Hegel, G. W. F. *The Philosophy of History.* New York: Dover, 1956.

The Hymnal 1940. New York: Church Hymnal Corporation, 1940.

Käsemann, Ernst. *Essays on New Testament Themes.* Philadelphia: Fortress Press, 1982.

————. *New Testament Questions of Today.* London: SCM Press, 1969.

Kant, Immanuel. "Beantwortung der Frage: Was ist Aufklärung." In *Was ist Aufklärung. Thesen und Definitionen.* Stuttgart: Reclam, 1974.

————. *Groundwork of the Metaphysic of Morals.* Translated and analysed by H. J. Patton. New York: Harper Torchbooks, 1964.

King, Stephen. *The Green Mile.* The Complete Serial Novel. New York, London, Toronto, Sydney, Tokyo, Singapore: Pocket Books, 1996.

Lake, Frank. "The Work of Christ in the Healing of Primal Pain." In *Theological Renewal* 6 (June/July 1977): 8-21.

Lewis, C. S. *The Lion, the Witch and the Wardrobe.* 1950; New York: Macmillan (Collier Books), 1970.

————. *The Last Battle.* 1956; New York: Macmillan (Collier Books), 1970.

Litton, E. A. *Introduction to Dogmatic Theology.* New edition. London: James Clarke & Co., 1960.

Luther's Vorreden zur Bibel. Edited by Heinrich Bornkamm. Göttingen: Vandenhoek & Ruprecht, 1989.

Moltmann, Jürgen. *Der gekreuzigte Gott. Das Kreuz Christi als Grund und Kritik Christlicher Theologie.* Sixth edition. Gütersloh: Chr. Kaiser/Gütersloher Verlagshaus, 1993.

————. *In der Geschichte der dreieinigen Gottes. Beiträge zur trinitarischen Theologie.* Munich: Chr. Kaiser Verlag, 1991.

————. "Justification and New Creation." In *The Future of Creation.* Philadelphia: Fortress Press, 1979.

————. "Protestantism: 'The Religion of Freedom.'" In *God for a Secular Society: The Public Relevance of Theology.* Minneapolis: Fortress Press, 1999.

Neef, Heinz-Dieter. *Die Prüfung Abrahams. Eine exegetisch — theologische Studie zu Gen 22,1-19.* Stuttgart: Calwer Verlag, 1998.

Newton, William Wilberforce. *Yesterday with the Fathers.* New York: Cochrane Publishing, 1910.

Stuhlmacher, Peter. *Biblische Theologie des Neuen Testaments.* Volume I. Göttingen: Vandenhoeck & Ruprecht, 1992.

————. *Was geschah auf Golgatha? Zur Heilsbedeutung von Kreuz, Tod und Auferweckung Jesu.* Stuttgart: Calwer Verlag, 1998.

Thomas, W. H. Griffith. *The Principles of Theology.* New edition. London: James Clarke & Co., 1960.

Weimer, Christoph. *Luther, Cranach und die Bilder, Gesetz und Evangelium — Schlüssel zum reformatorischen Bildgebrauch.* Stuttgart: Calwer Verlag, 1999.

Zahl, Paul F. M. *Die Rechtfertigungslehre Ernst Käsemanns.* Calwer Theologische Monographien, Reihe B: Systematische Theologie und Kirchengeschichte, vol. 13. Stuttgart: Calwer Verlag, 1996.

Index of Authors

INDEX OF AUTHORS

Index of Biblical References